ALSO BY J. M. HIRSCH

SHAKE STRAIN DONE: CRAFT COCKTAILS AT HOME

POUR ME ANOTHER

250 WAYS TO FIND YOUR FAVORITE DRINK

J. M. HIRSCH

ILLUSTRATIONS BY LIKA KVIRIKASHVILI

VORACIOUS

LITTLE, BROWN AND COMPANY

NEW YORK BOSTON LONDON

Voracious
Little, Brown and Company
Hachette Book Group
1290 Avenue of the Americas, New York, NY 10104
littlebrown.com

First Edition: October 2022

Voracious is an imprint of Little, Brown and Company, a division of Hachette Book Group, Inc. The Voracious name and logo are trademarks of Hachette Book Group, Inc.

The publisher is not responsible for websites (or their content) that are not owned by the publisher.

The Hachette Speakers Bureau provides a wide range of authors for speaking events. To find out more, go to hachettespeakersbureau.com or call (866) 376-6591.

Illustrations by Lika Kvirikashvili

ISBN 9780316325356
Library of Congress Control Number: 2022936660

10 9 8 7 6 5 4 3 2 1

LSC-C

Printed in the United States of America

CONTENTS

CHOOSE YOUR OWN COCKTAIL ADVENTURE

START WITH WHAT YOU KNOW.
DISCOVER WHAT YOU LOVE.

That's *Pour Me Another,* a choose-your-own-adventure guide to the world of cocktails. This book is a simple and intuitive way to make delicious drinking discoveries, starting from the liquors and cocktails you are most familiar with. Because the drinks you already know you like are just the beginning.

One of the fascinating aspects of cocktails is the unexpected ways that liquors can be transformed depending on how and with what they are mixed. These transformations give us the space to experiment with and discover the drinks we never knew we would enjoy.

This is where "I don't like tequila" becomes "I like tequila *when*..."

Each chapter focuses on a single liquor and begins with its most recognizable cocktail. A tequila Margarita. A Gin and Tonic. A rum Daiquiri. A Vodka Martini. A bourbon Old Fashioned.

From each of those iconic drinks, every chapter explores 50 iterations, tracing the ways the base liquor evolves in the shaker, in the glass and on our tongues. From the comfort of the drinks we know—which present their liquors in such familiar ways—we branch and explore, discovering the many and varied ways each liquor can express itself. We follow each from its lightest and most refreshing to its most bold and brooding.

Many of the recipes are modern interpretations of classics—some forgotten—drawn from mixology's deep archives. The modern cocktail is a craft some 200 or more years old and its history is rich with the wisdom of bartenders such as Harry Craddock, Tom Bullock, David Embury, Harry MacElhone, Robert Vermeire, Jerry Thomas, Charles H. Baker Jr. and many others.

To find the right recipes for this exploration, I dived deep into the booze-stained texts of those pillars of mixology, simplifying, amplifying, standardizing and modernizing. The result is an almost Socratic exploration of gin, rum, tequila and mezcal, vodka, and bourbon and rye, all grounded in history.

You might know what to expect from gin, for example. Take a sip. What do you get? Depending on the bundle of botanicals with which it was made, likely piney-resinous notes backed by some herbaceous elements and faint sweetness.

Try it in the classic Gin and Tonic. The gently bitter quinine of tonic water—not to mention its sugar and effervescence—balance the spice and strength of the gin, letting it take a refreshing turn. All of this we expect. Perhaps you like it, or maybe not.

Now try a Bijou, a cocktail that dates to the late 1800s and delivers gin in a form reminiscent of a Manhattan. That's the sweet vermouth and herbaceous Green Chartreuse talking. The resulting cocktail is herbal, warm and creamy. And if you're typically more of a whiskey drinker, suddenly you have an open door to exploring gin.

We can run this spectrum with each of the liquors in this book. A bourbon Old Fashioned, for example, takes a sweet and herbal turn when the addition of sweet vermouth changes it into a Manhattan. Add Campari to get a sweetly bitter—and pleasantly strong—Boulevardier. Want something stronger? Lose the Campari in favor of Bénédictine and cognac (upping the herbal and sweet notes) and now you've got a deliciously potent Vieux Carré.

All of those drinks exist in a similar flavor sphere. But it's easy to take bourbon in entirely different directions. Starting back at the Old Fashioned, lose the bitters in favor of lemon to make a Whiskey Sour, a cocktail that is an entirely different experience. The Brown Derby switches in honey for the sugar and grapefruit juice for the lemon. Still sour and sweet, but nothing like a Whiskey Sour.

The story plays out similarly for vodka, agave liquors (tequila and mezcal) and rum. Take the Mojito, a lightly sweet and herbal way to sip rum. There's plenty to love. But you'd never mistake it for a spicy, peppery-sweet Dark and Stormy. Or for a sweet and sour Daiquiri. In fact, the Daiquiri has more in common with a tequila Margarita and a Whiskey Sour than most other rum drinks. And vodka? It's the true chameleon of the liquor world. You can take it anywhere from a bright and tart Cosmopolitan to a rich and velvety Espresso Martini.

All of which makes clear, the liquors we love—and those we think we don't—can wear many guises. The more we explore their range, the more new drinks we can find to enjoy.

Like my book *Shake Strain Done: Craft Cocktails at Home,* these recipes are written in a language you can taste. Each cocktail is described with a spectrum of terms that we understand long before our lips ever touch the glass.

Every cocktail is identified by some combination of characteristics—**REFRESH-ING, CREAMY, FRUITY, SWEET, SOUR, HERBAL, BITTER, SPICY, SMOKY, WARM** and **STRONG**. This not only communicates what's in the glass, it also helps identify relationships between cocktails that may seem quite different on the surface, but in fact offer similar constellations of flavors.

So let's get to it. Let's start with what we know. And let's discover what we love.

START WITH WHAT YOU KNOW, DISCOVER WHAT YOU LOVE

I wrote this book because I've suffered through too many cocktails that sound great on paper, only to disappoint in the glass. The point of *Pour Me Another* is to take the guesswork out of finding drinks you'll enjoy, even if you've never sipped something similar and know little about the ingredients used to make it. You can approach the book three ways.

DIVE RIGHT IN

Just start flipping pages. In addition to history and tasting notes, every cocktail is described using evocative terms, words we can taste without having ever sipped the cocktail.

For every recipe, you'll see a combination of traits—REFRESHING, CREAMY, FRUITY, SWEET, SOUR, HERBAL, BITTER, SPICY, SMOKY, WARM and STRONG—ordered from boldest to faintest to indicate what to expect. Not sure if you're a NEGRONI drinker? You might be, if you enjoy drinks that are BITTER, REFRESHING and a touch FRUITY.

These flavor characteristics also reveal the relationships between drinks, making it easy to find similar cocktails to enjoy. At the bottom of every recipe, you'll see a list of suggested drinks to try next. If you like the BITTER, REFRESHING and FRUITY notes of a gin NEGRONI, chances are you'll also enjoy a BITTER, SWEET and FRUITY tequila-based LA ROSITA.

DRINK PROGRESSIVELY

The drinks in each chapter are ordered from mildest to boldest. Are you a tequila drinker hankering for something with oomph? Start your exploration toward the back of the chapter, where you'll find recipes with STRONG and SMOKY notes. Prefer something REFRESHING and SWEET? You belong at the beginning.

This structure also demonstrates how a liquor can change and express itself in different cocktails. You may think you're not a bourbon drinker because you don't like the STRONG and WARM notes of an OLD FASHIONED. But maybe you'd enjoy bourbon's FRUITY, SWEET and SOUR side in the BROWN DERBY.

START WITH THE CLASSICS

Still not sure where to start? The following pages list 10 of the most popular classic cocktails ordered at bars. After each, I've offered drinks that have similar taste profiles. This makes it simple to start with something familiar and use it to find something new, different and even more delicious.

IF YOU LIKE **THE APEROL SPRITZ** YOU'RE GOING TO LOVE …

Your basic **APEROL SPRITZ**–Aperol, prosecco and a slice of orange–
is a bright little bomb of SWEET, BITTER, REFRESHING and just a tiny bit FRUITY.

 You'll get much of the same from a **MR. 404** (p. 100), which loses the prosecco in favor of vodka and pairs the Aperol with floral elderflower liqueur, as well as both lemon and orange.

 If that's too much for you, try an **AGAVE SPRITZ** (p. 276), which builds your basic Aperol Spritz, but tosses in some SMOKY reposado tequila.

 For a creamier take on that, try an **AMBER ON THE ROCKS** (p. 87), which keeps the vodka and Aperol, but adds CREAMY via some vanilla-spice Licor 43.

 An **OLD PAL** (p. 62) pairs gin and Aperol, along with grapefruit, lemon and elderflower liqueur for a cocktail that's BITTER, SWEET and FRUITY.

 Or opt for **LA ROSITA** (p. 275), which brings you closer to a Negroni with BITTER, SWEET, FRUITY and a dash of SMOKY notes from a combination of Campari, sweet vermouth and orange bitters.

 THE RED DEVIL (p. 257) ups the FRUITY with mango. It also ups the BITTER by swapping stronger Campari for the Aperol.

IF YOU LIKE **THE DAIQUIRI** YOU'RE GOING TO LOVE ...

If your drink of choice is the basic rum DAIQUIRI (p. 183),
chances are you favor cocktails that are strongly SWEET and SOUR,
thanks to its hefty helpings of sugar and lime juice.

Start with a classic, stay with a classic. The MARGARITA (p. 235) is for you. Tequila stands in for the rum and a splash of orange liqueur adds FRUITY and SWEET notes to complement the lime.

A GIN RICKEY (p. 53) returns to lime, but gets much of its sweetness from FRUITY apricot brandy. A splash of club soda adds a nice effervescence that lightens everything.

Staying on that theme, try an AL PASTOR MARGARITA (p. 262), which adds basil, cilantro and pineapple to the mix for HERBAL and SWEET accents.

Still with gin, a SALTY DOG (p. 54) opts for grapefruit over lime, and leans on elderflower liqueur for the floral SWEET notes.

The BENNETT (p. 44) is pretty much a Daiquiri, but with gin and a splash of dry vermouth, the latter letting the lime shine a little brighter.

If you're feeling tropical, grab some vodka and coconut water for a LIME IN DE COCONUT (p. 83), which adds CREAMY to the mix of SWEET and SOUR.

Sticking with gin, try a BEE'S KNEES (p. 52), which swaps floral honey for the traditional sugar syrup and lemon for the lime. My version also adds ginger liqueur for a bee sting kick.

Not to be left out, whiskey edges into the category with THE BROWN DERBY (p. 134), which blends bourbon, grapefruit and honey.

IF YOU LIKE **THE ESPRESSO MARTINI** YOU'RE GOING TO LOVE ...

Done right, the ESPRESSO MARTINI (p. 123) is gloriously STRONG, CREAMY, BITTER and ever-so-slightly SWEET. It should contain nothing more than vodka, Kahlúa and freshly brewed espresso.

The easy transition is to try a COFFEE CARGO COCKTAIL (p. 122), which takes that basic equation and adds a scoop of vanilla ice cream. Indulgent as all (expletive deleted).

Likewise, THE MULE'S HIND LEG (p. 65) hits those beautiful STRONG and CREAMY notes with a combination of gin, Bénédictine, cognac and maple syrup.

Or mix things up with a FRANGELIC BEAUTY (p. 106), which adds Frangelico—a hazelnut liqueur—and a bit of sugar syrup to the mix. The result is SWEET, CREAMY and STRONG.

But if STRONG and CREAMY is your thing, consider a PIÑA COLADA (p. 192). It lacks the intensity of the Espresso Martini, but delivers plenty of its smooth sipping.

Somehow, the AZTEC'S MARK (p. 154) manages to achieve the same flavor spectrum, but via a blend of bourbon, crème de cacao, Bénédictine and mildly spicy Ancho Reyes chili liqueur.

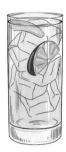

IF YOU LIKE **THE GIN AND TONIC** YOU'RE GOING TO LOVE ...

The classic GIN AND TONIC (p. 27) is straightforward, delivering a clean REFRESH-ING note, along with gentle SWEET and SOUR from the tonic and lime. Depending on your pour (and quality) of tonic, you also can get some BITTER from the quinine.

 For a FRUITY take, go with a **CHERRY-LIME VODKA RICKEY** (p. 109), which adds cherry syrup and seltzer to the equation.

 If you'd rather stick with gin, there is a **PUNCH À LA FORD** (p. 32). It swaps lemon for the lime, bitters for the quinine and tosses in some white rum.

 Similarly, **THE RUM AND THE RESTLESS** (p. 190) delivers tropical refreshing notes by pairing the lime with white rum, crème de cacao, coconut water and honey.

 Or lean in on that theme with a **LIME IN DE COCONUT** (p. 83), which pairs the lime and coconut water with SPICY ginger liqueur and vodka.

 For a slightly more HERBAL take, try a **BENNETT** (p. 44). The lime and gin stay, but dry vermouth and bitters give it a touch of sophistication.

 A **BEE'S KNEES** (p. 52) swaps lemon for lime and sweetens things up with honey. Ginger liqueur and orange bitters keep things bright and SPICY.

 A **NAVY GROG** (p. 222) takes a darker turn, combining white and aged rums. The lime gets some citrus help from grapefruit, and honey ensures the BITTER is balanced with SWEET.

IF YOU LIKE **THE MANHATTAN** YOU'RE GOING TO LOVE ...

The MANHATTAN (p. 153) is a classic that's easy to love. With either rye or bourbon, plus sweet vermouth, bitters and a maraschino cherry, you get plenty of WARM, STRONG, SWEET and SPICY notes. And there are endless ways to achieve similar profiles.

The easiest, of course, is to simply leave out the sweet vermouth, which creates another classic, the slightly less SWEET OLD FASHIONED (p. 131).

Or ditch the whiskey entirely and make a MARTINEZ (p. 74), which pretty much amounts to a gin Manhattan, which is STRONG, HERBAL and SWEET.

Or you could swap dry vermouth for the sweet vermouth and make a DRY MANHATTAN (p. 149), which is less SWEET and more HERBAL.

If rum is more your thing, try a POKER COCKTAIL (p. 226), which—you guessed it—is pretty much a white rum Manhattan.

A NARRAGANSETT (p. 146) keeps the basic equation, but uses a bit of anise-rich absinthe in place of the bitters. The result is wonderfully balanced.

Want to up the STRONG and WARM? You need a VIEUX CARRÉ (p. 180), which blends rye, sweet vermouth, cognac and the HERBAL notes of Bénédictine.

A MAKE YOUR MARK (p. 76) takes your classic Manhattan and adds botanical richness with a bit of gin.

IF YOU LIKE **THE MARGARITA** YOU'RE GOING TO LOVE ...

Built from blanco tequila, lime juice, orange liqueur and sugar, the classic
MARGARITA (p. 235) drinks similar to the Daiquiri with strong SWEET and SOUR
notes, but ratchets up the FRUITY and REFRESHING side of things.

 So if you're moving on from a Margarita, you can just drink a DAIQUIRI (p. 183), which pares it down and subs rum. Nothing wrong with that.

 The NAKED AND FAMOUS (p. 264) adds HERBAL Yellow Chartreuse and gently BITTER Aperol to the blend.

 But if you want to stick with agave-based liquors, try a TEQUILA PONCHA (p. 252), which uses honey instead of sugar syrup, and a blend of orange, grapefruit and lemon in place of the lime.

 For an HERBAL take, try a TEQUILA MOJITO (p. 269), which pretty much is a tequila-based Daiquiri with ample mint added to the action.

 As with the Daiquiri, the AL PASTOR MARGARITA (p. 262) makes a fine alternative. It adds basil, cilantro and pineapple to the mix for HERBAL and SWEET accents.

 And wrap up with a switch back to rum with a NAVY GROG (p. 222), which blends white and aged rums with honey, grapefruit and lime.

 Or lean SMOKY with a TAMARIND MARGARITA (p. 263), which keeps the Margarita's orange liqueur and lime juice, but adds tart tamarind and spicy ancho chili powder to the mix.

IF YOU LIKE **THE MOJITO** YOU'RE GOING TO LOVE ...

With ample mint, lime and white rum, the classic MOJITO (p. 186) packs plenty of
REFRESHING, SWEET and HERBAL notes, with just a hint of SOUR from the lime.

You could keep things light by making a TEQUILA MOJITO (p. 269), which brings a little SMOKY to the picture by using tequila instead of rum.

Or keep it simple with a MINT FIZZ (p. 126), which loses the lime in favor of lemon and a splash of club soda.

Staying on that path, an AGUA DE TOMATILLO (p. 237) ups the SOUR by mixing in tangy tomatillos along with the lime.

Prefer brown liquors? Try a MINT JULEP (p. 165), which delivers STRONG, SWEET and HERBAL via a mix of mint, bourbon and bitters.

Switching to vodka, now try a VODKA CAIPIRINHA (p. 115). It has all the lime and mint you want, but also adds some SPICY ginger liqueur.

IF YOU LIKE **THE NEGRONI** YOU'RE GOING TO LOVE ...

Gin **NEGRONI** (p. 61) drinkers like their cocktails BITTER and REFRESHING, with hints of FRUITY. There is lots of room to explore from there.

The **BOULEVARDIER** (p. 150) takes the Negroni in a new direction, replacing the classic gin with rye for a BITTER, STRONG and SWEET sipper.

Or try **LA ROSITA** (p. 275), which pretty much is a tequila Negroni that delivers BITTER, SWEET and FRUITY notes from a combination of Campari, sweet vermouth and dry vermouth.

THE RED DEVIL (p. 257) sticks with the tequila, but replaces the traditional notes of orange with mango.

The **JUNGLE BIRD** (p. 225) follows a similar equation, but opts for white rum and pineapple with lime for the FRUITY notes.

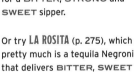

Meanwhile, the **OLD PAL** (p. 62) heads back to gin, but opts for a blend of grapefruit and elderflower liqueur to deliver the SWEET and FRUITY side. It also eases up on the BITTER by opting for Aperol over Campari.

The **AGAVE SPRITZ** (p. 276) returns us to tequila territory, now punched up with Aperol to deliver a cocktail that's something between a Negroni and an Aperol Spritz.

And not to leave out vodka, you could try an **AMBER ON THE ROCKS** (p. 87), which gets its SWEET and BITTER notes from vanilla-spice Licor 43 and Aperol.

IF YOU LIKE   THE OLD FASHIONED   YOU'RE GOING TO LOVE ...

If you drink a whiskey OLD FASHIONED (p. 131), chances are you like drinks that are STRONG and WARM with hints of SWEET, SPICY and maybe a dash of FRUITY. Where to go from there?

 One obvious choice, of course, is the MANHATTAN (p. 153), which adds sweet vermouth to your classic Old Fashioned of whiskey, sugar and bitters.

 For a simpler take, go with a VODKA OLD FASHIONED (p. 124), which plays out STRONG, FRUITY and SWEET.

 From there, you could go with a POKER COCKTAIL (p. 226), which is pretty much a Manhattan in which white rum stands in for the whiskey.

 A gin-based BIJOU (p. 58) on paper seems nothing like any of these—gin, sweet vermouth and Green Chartreuse—yet drinks like a cross between an Old Fashioned and a Manhattan.

 For a middle ground there is a MISSISSIPPI PUNCH (p. 232), which blends bourbon, rum and sweet vermouth to bring you close to a Manhattan, but with a slightly sweeter side.

 Or try a VIEUX CARRÉ (p. 180), which lives somewhere between an Old Fashioned and a Manhattan thanks to the addition of sweet vermouth, cognac and Bénédictine.

 A RUM OLD FASHIONED (p. 229) replaces the whiskey with white and aged rums, creating a cocktail that is STRONG, CREAMY and SWEET.

IF YOU LIKE **THE VODKA MARTINI** YOU'RE GOING TO LOVE ...

With just vodka, dry vermouth and (maybe) green olives, the VODKA MARTINI (p. 79)
doesn't give us a lot to work with. It's STRONG with (if made properly) only the
barest hints of HERBAL and SWEET. Yet, there's still room to explore.

Start by going back to the
cocktail's roots, the GIN MARTINI
(p. 75). It's the same equation
(though I like mine with orange
bitters), subbing gin. The result
is more HERBAL thanks to the
botanicals of the gin.

Add some sparkling wine to the
Vodka Old Fashioned and now
you've got a CANCAN (p. 85),
which brings gentle SWEET notes
to this otherwise potent equation.

From there, try a TUXEDO (p. 39),
which adds dashes of absinthe and
maraschino liqueur to up the
HERBAL, SWEET and—surprisingly—
CREAMY notes ever so slightly.

The FRENCH MARTINI (p. 104) takes
things decidedly SWEET with the
addition of pineapple and raspberry
liqueur.

The VODKA OLD FASHIONED (p. 124)
pares things down, losing the dry
vermouth and olives in favor of
bitters and a strip of orange zest.

And if you're willing to abandon
vodka, try a CHOKER COCKTAIL
(p. 148), which stays STRONG
and HERBAL thanks to a
combination of bourbon, absinthe
and orange bitters.

MIXOLOGY, MY WAY

I'm not a fan of kitchen sinking a cocktail, tossing in a muddle of ingredients that obscure the key flavors. Mixology, like cooking, is best when balanced. This means the ingredients you leave out can be just as important as those you put in.

Lemon, for example. In some cocktails, the juice obliterates with acidity. It's why I often instead use lemon zest, its aromatic oils delivering potent flavor without souring the drink. Sweeteners, too. Almost always less than more, the former rounding the drink, the latter dulling it.

It's what I call delicious minimalism, an insistence that every ingredient earn its keep by making the whole greater without dominating. It also means combining flavors in ways that complement one another and create a gentle push and pull on the tongue. Sweet and sour. Spicy and creamy.

Likewise, I want to taste the liquor I'm drinking. There's a lot happening even in a basic Gin and Tonic. I want to taste those botanicals and the sweetly bitter quinine. In an Old Fashioned, please spare me the fruit salad. I want to focus on the interplay of bourbon and bitters.

Many of the cocktails in this book are drawn from the annals of mixology, recipe collections that reach to the dawn of the craft in the early 1800s. Some of those early drinks were masterful, setting in motion generations of fine libations.

Others had solid bones, but were...a bit confused. It's no one's fault. Our ingredients have come far since those times. Especially during and following Prohibition, drinks often were created to purposefully mask the flavor of lesser liquors.

Thankfully, we no longer need to hide the bathtub booze. So reviving some of these classic recipes meant paring them back, simplifying them so the delicious inspiration that birthed them so long ago can truly shine.

Finally, a note about salt. You'll notice that many of the recipes in this book call for 6 to 10 granules of kosher salt. Not for the rim of the glass. But to stir or shake into the drink itself.

Salt, just as in cooking, elevates and rounds out all the other flavors in a cocktail. It won't taste briny, but it will leave the drink tasting fuller and brighter. Do a side-by-side with your favorite cocktail—with salt and without—and you'll be shocked by the difference.

Professional mixologists do this all the time, often using saline solutions, which they add to cocktails by using droppers. If you want to try this, mix 4 grams kosher salt with 96 grams water until dissolved. Use ¼ to ½ teaspoon of this saline per cocktail.

That said, I find that with most stirred or shaken cocktails, you can skip the saline step and simply add salt granules directly to the drink. They'll dissolve without much trouble.

GIN

Gin—essentially a neutral liquor that's been infused with tons of botanical goodness, particularly juniper—really is the old-timer of the cocktail world. Many of the first true cocktails used it as the base. This provides us with plenty of history from which to unearth inspiration. It also is a liquor that is surprisingly versatile. Sure, it can drink as a REFRESHING, SWEET and SOUR GIN AND TONIC. But it also can get all gussied up as a BIJOU, which drinks almost like a MANHATTAN thanks to Green Chartreuse and sweet vermouth. In between, you've got the CREAMY POET'S DREAM, which adds Bénédictine and dry vermouth. Add some orange liqueur to that and now you've got a FRUITY and SWEET SATAN'S WHISKERS. Meanwhile, THE HORSE THIEF adds absinthe to get us some strong HERBAL notes. And then, of course, you go all BITTER once you add Campari to make a NEGRONI.

There are plenty of styles of gin, with genever, Old Tom, and London or American dry being the most common. Genever is a distant cousin from the modern stuff. It has an earthy, smoky flavor that makes it ill suited as an everyday mixer. Old Tom is a bit sweeter than genever and has less botanical action than what most of us expect in a gin. In general, your best bet for mixing cocktails will be a London dry or an American dry. For the latter, I like Aviation. For a slightly more juniper take on it, Branchwater is lovely, too.

GIN AND TONIC

The Gin and Tonic dates to at least the early 1800s, when officers in the British East India Company drank quinine-spiked water to prevent malaria. To make the bitter tonic water more palatable, they often diluted it with gin. Got to love any soldier who uses high-proof booze to dilute flavored water. Though quinine mostly was debunked as a means of preventing malaria (at least at the concentrations in a beverage), the combination stuck.

The beauty of the Gin and Tonic is that the recipe is contained in the name. Except that doesn't quite capture the complexity that presents in the glass. First, you have the gin, which brings bold botanical notes, notably juniper and coriander. Then the tonic water, which combines bitter quinine and a fair amount of sugar. The tonic water also offers a gentle effervescence, that last bit enhancing the aromatic nature of everything else. A bit of ice offers dilution, which opens up the gin, allowing us to appreciate more of what's under the hood.

Because of its simplicity, a good Gin and Tonic relies heavily on getting the proportions right. Most recipes call for a 1:2 ratio of gin to tonic water. I find that lacking, the quinine and sugar overpowering the botanical notes of the gin. I prefer the more balanced flavors of using nearly equal parts gin and tonic water.

POUR ME ANOTHER

★ NOW TRY ★

The Rum and the Restless, 190
Lime in de Coconut, 83
Cherry-Lime Vodka Rickey, 109
Punch à la Ford, 32
Bennett, 44
Bee's Knees, 52
Navy Grog, 222

3 ounces gin

4 ounces tonic water

1 lime wedge

1 lemon zest strip

Ice cubes

In a highball glass, stir together the gin and tonic water. Squeeze the lime wedge into the drink, then add it, the lemon zest strip and ample ice. Stir gently.

HEMINGWAY DAIQUIRI NO. 2

The Hemingway Daiquiri—named for the man who supposedly drank too many of them—can be a slushy-sweet mess of white rum, maraschino liqueur, ample lime juice and a bit of grapefruit juice. Death & Co's Alex Day tamed that cocktail to create the High Five, which substitutes gin for the rum and Aperol for the maraschino, a liquor that can be one-note sweet. My take on the Hemingway Daiquiri further refines the equation by dropping the lime juice—which competes with the grapefruit juice. Upping the gin and Aperol and limiting the lime to a zest strip retains the flavor profile, but keeps each ingredient distinct and clear.

1 lime zest strip

2 ounces gin

1 ounce Aperol

¼ ounce grapefruit juice

¼ ounce agave or simple syrup

6 to 10 granules kosher salt

Ice cubes

Rub the lime zest strip around the rim of a coupe, then add it to the glass. In a cocktail shaker, combine the gin, Aperol, grapefruit juice, syrup and salt. Shake with ice cubes, then strain into the coupe.

POUR ME ANOTHER

★ NOW TRY ★

Old Pal, 62
Orange Bat, 184
Naked and Famous, 264

ARMY AND NAVY

REFRESHING

FRUITY

SWEET

SOUR

The classic Army and Navy cocktail dates to around World War II. The original was a gin sour in which the typical simple syrup was replaced by orgeat, an almond-based sweetener that often includes orange flower water. This version instead uses falernum, a similarly viscous syrup that brings flavors of almond, ginger and lime, as well as warm spices. A bit of orange liqueur ensures we don't lose the orange notes and—contrary to tradition—we serve it over crushed ice, which keeps the sour and sweet notes from overwhelming the drink.

2 ounces gin

½ ounce orange liqueur

¼ ounce falernum syrup

¼ ounce lemon juice

6 to 10 granules kosher salt

Ice, cubes and crushed

In a cocktail shaker, combine the gin, orange liqueur, falernum, lemon juice and salt. Shake with ice cubes. Strain into a coupe filled halfway with crushed ice.

POUR ME ANOTHER
★ NOW TRY ★

Opium, 236
Bay Breeze, 80
Tiki Tundra, 81
Between the Sheets, 185

FRENCH 75

The ancestors of the French 75—a spritely mix of gin, lemon juice, simple syrup and sparkling wine—have been around since at least the 1860s, when Jerry Thomas concocted the *Bartender's Guide: How to Mix Drinks.* He has two drinks—the Champagne Cocktail and the Gin Cocktail—which over time seem to have merged their best elements. By 1922, Robert Vermeire's *Cocktails: How to Mix Them* included a gussied-up version that combined gin, calvados, lemon juice and grenadine. Bartenders have been refining it ever since.

In this version, I opt to keep the flavors simple and clean, the best bet for letting the gin and sparkling wine play together and accentuate one another. Many modern takes on the French 75 favor a ratio of just a bit of gin to copious sparkling wine. I lean more to the gin, which brings so much more to the table. I also swap lemon zest muddled with sugar over lemon juice, as the latter tends to dominate.

2 lemon zest strips

½ teaspoon white sugar

2 ounces gin

⅛ ounce (¾ teaspoon) orange liqueur

Dash Angostura bitters

Ice cubes

3 ounces sparkling wine

In a cocktail shaker, muddle 1 lemon zest strip and the sugar. Add the gin, orange liqueur and bitters. Shake with ice cubes. Strain into a coupe. Top with sparkling wine. Stir gently, then squeeze the remaining lemon zest strip over the glass and add it to the cocktail.

POUR ME ANOTHER

★ NOW TRY ★

Cancan, 85
Army and Navy, 29
Bay Breeze, 80
Tiki Tundra, 81
Between the Sheets, 185
Opium, 236

THE JOURNALIST

Harry Craddock of London's The Savoy hotel often is credited with first printing the recipe for this brooding, yet bright cocktail in his 1930 classic, *The Savoy Cocktail Book*. But the honor actually goes to a different Harry. Harry MacElhone included a version in his early 1920s *Harry's ABC of Mixing Cocktails*. Both men favored a generous glug of gin married to light—but equal—touches of sweet and dry vermouths, as well as dashes of lemon juice, orange liqueur and Angostura bitters. I took my cue from a different generation—Jim Meehan. His version ups the orange liqueur and lemon juice to equal the vermouths. I followed his lead on the liqueur, but left the lemon juice at a dash. Be warned—this one is a silent killer. It drinks smooth and clear.

2 ounces gin

½ ounce dry vermouth

½ ounce sweet vermouth

½ ounce orange liqueur

Dash lemon juice

Dash Angostura bitters

Ice cubes

In a cocktail shaker, combine the gin, both vermouths, the orange liqueur, lemon juice and bitters. Shake with ice cubes, then strain into a coupe.

POUR ME ANOTHER

★ NOW TRY ★

Dunlop, 219

PUNCH À LA FORD

This lightly sweet cocktail dates to the mid-1800s, when a General Ford (No, not that one. Or that one.) apparently made it in great quantities, then aged it in his basement. The classic version—spelled out first in Benson Hill's *The Epicure's Almanac* and later in Jerry Thomas' 1862 *Bartender's Guide*—called for lemon syrup, cognac and Jamaica rum. It also could be made with gin, at which point it was creatively renamed Gin Punch. For a scaled-down version, I opted for the best elements of both, combining the gin and rum with lemon and just a hint of sugar. The salt and Angostura bitters aren't traditional, but they do a wonderful job balancing and rounding out the other flavors.

1 lemon zest strip

Ice, cubes and crushed

2 ounces gin

1 ounce white rum

¼ ounce agave or simple syrup

6 to 10 granules kosher salt

Dash Angostura bitters

Rub the zest along the rim of a coupe, then add it to the glass. Fill the coupe halfway with crushed ice. In a cocktail shaker, combine the gin, rum, syrup, bitters and salt. Shake with ice cubes, then strain into the coupe.

POUR ME ANOTHER

★ NOW TRY ★

Mai Tai, 189

The Rum and the Restless, 190

GIMLET

REFRESHING

SOUR

SWEET

Back in the day, sailors weren't the healthiest lot. Scurvy and all, among their many concerns. Over the years, a variety of solutions were tried to get the men their vitamin C while at sea. One was to combine lime juice and sugar, creating the original lime cordial. Since the same sailors also were fond of their gin, it wasn't long before the Gimlet was born. Most recipes called for a blend of lime cordial and gin, often in equal or near equal parts. In *The Gentleman's Companion,* Charles H. Baker Jr. adds a generous dash of "chilled plain water" to the mix, presumably to tame the cordial, which he described as "pungent." I'm in his corner. But rather than dilute the cocktail, I took a different tack, one that preserves the bold lime flavor and sweetness without overwhelming the gin. Muddling lime zest with sugar syrup delivers the same bright flavor minus the potent acidity of the juice. Consider it a kinder, gentler Gimlet.

2-inch strip lime zest

¼ ounce agave or simple syrup

2½ ounces gin

Ice cubes

1 lime round

POUR ME ANOTHER

★ NOW TRY ★

Lime in de Coconut, 83

In a cocktail shaker, combine the lime zest and syrup. Aggressively muddle the zest; leave the muddler in the shaker. Add the gin, then swish the muddler to rinse; remove the muddler. Shake with ice cubes, then strain into a cocktail glass. Float the lime round in the cocktail.

SOUTHSIDE

Consider the Southside the naughty sibling of the Gimlet. The drink—a blend of lemon or lime juice, sugar and gin spiked with fresh mint—can be traced back to at least the early 1900s, when rumor suggests it was the favored cocktail of Al Capone, who lorded over Chicago's South Side. During Prohibition, New York's 21 Club speakeasy pushed the Southside cocktail from the mobsters to the masses.

Over the years, there have been many iterations of the Southside, including some that grew into separate cocktails entirely. In 1930, Harry Craddock wrote about the Fallen Angel, which delivers the same basic flavor profile, but gets its mint and sugar from crème de menthe. If you add soda water to the basic formula you create a Southside Fizz. Add sparkling wine and you have a Southside Royale.

As with the Gimlet (p. 33), here I favor citrus zest over juice. This allows the bright flavor of the fruit to permeate the drink without overwhelming the other flavors with sour acidity. For fun, I use a strip of zest from both lemon and lime, but feel free to use just one or the other. The muddling in this cocktail occurs in two stages—first the zest, which needs a firm hand, then the mint, which prefers a gentler touch.

1-inch strip lime zest
1-inch strip lemon zest
¼ ounce agave or simple syrup
5 fresh mint leaves, plus 1 large
to garnish

2½ ounces gin
Dash Angostura bitters
Ice cubes

In a cocktail shaker, combine the lime and lemon zests and syrup. Aggressively muddle the zests. Add the mint and gently muddle again. Leave the muddler in the shaker. Add the gin, then swish the muddler to rinse; remove the muddler. Add the bitters. Shake with ice cubes, then double strain into a cocktail glass.

POUR ME ANOTHER

★ NOW TRY ★

Death in the Gulfstream, 56

GIN FIZZ

CREAMY
REFRESHING
SOUR
SWEET

The Fizz—an offshoot of the Sour family, a class of drinks built from a liquor, citrus juice and a sweetener—has a long and spiraling lineage. The most basic Fizz—of which the Gin Fizz is the most common—goes back to at least the 1860s, when Jerry Thomas offered up a Gin Fix, a blend of liquor, lemon juice and sugar finished with some variety of carbonated water. In time, that bred the Silver Fizz, which added a frothy egg white to the mix. By the end of that century, Henry Ramos had created the New Orleans Fizz (now simply called the Ramos Gin Fizz), which elevated—quite literally—the basic fizz with both lime juice and lemon juice, egg white, heavy cream and orange flower water, the result featuring a thick layer of foam that floats to the top of the glass. There are many stories of the shaking showmanship of this iteration. Ramos supposedly employed as many as a dozen bartenders to shake each cocktail, passing it one to another for a full 12 minutes of shaking.

Though I liked Ramos' combination of lemon and lime, I found that the cream—even when scaled back from the 1 ounce he used—dulled and diluted the other flavors. So I left that out, creating something of a hybrid between his version and the Silver Fizz. I also opted for more common orange liqueur over harder to find orange water.

POUR ME ANOTHER

✳ NOW TRY ✳

Mint Fizz, 126
Pink Lady, 40

3 ounces gin
½ ounce egg white
¼ ounce orange liqueur
¼ ounce lemon juice
¼ ounce lime juice

¼ ounce agave or simple syrup
6 to 10 granules kosher salt
Ice cubes
Splash seltzer water

In a cocktail shaker, combine the gin, egg white, orange liqueur, lemon juice, lime juice, syrup and salt. Dry shake without ice for 20 seconds. Add ice cubes, then shake for 10 seconds. Strain into a coupe. Add a splash of seltzer.

THE POET'S DREAM

The Poet's Dream was born as a mix of equal parts gin-dry vermouth-Bénédictine, first appearing in *The Old Waldorf-Astoria Bar Book* in 1935. It had no bitters and—despite the ease of the equation—no balance. This version puts it all in perspective, letting the gin take the lead while the vermouth and Bénédictine offer supporting roles. The orgeat adds sweetness and body to what otherwise can feel very much like a Martini. The orange bitters and zest strip keep everything feeling light and bright.

1 orange zest strip

2 ounces gin

¾ ounce dry vermouth

½ ounce Bénédictine

⅛ ounce (¾ teaspoon) orgeat syrup

Dash orange bitters

Ice cubes

Rub the zest around the rim of a coupe, then add it to the glass. In a cocktail shaker, combine the gin, vermouth, Bénédictine, orgeat and bitters. Shake with ice cubes. Strain into the coupe.

POUR ME ANOTHER

★ NOW TRY ★

Gypsy Queen, 89
Spiced Orange Daiquiri, 193
Jungle Bird, 225
Toronjil, 241
The Fitzroy, 239

THE AVIATION

The Aviation dates to at least the early 1900s and traditionally is a floral mix of gin, maraschino liqueur, crème de violette and a whole lot of lemon juice. The gin and maraschino play well together, but crème de violette and lemon almost always overpower them, resulting in a cocktail that tastes like sucking on a lemon-soaked bouquet of wildflowers. This version tames the unruly elements by swapping lemon zest for the juice—you keep the bright citrus notes without adding all that acid—and ditches the perfume-like crème de violette for a lightly sweet, gently spicy blend of Lillet Blanc and Bénédictine. The sophisticated side of taking flight.

Lemon zest strip

2 ounces gin

¼ ounce maraschino liqueur

½ ounce Bénédictine

¼ ounce Lillet Blanc

6 to 10 granules kosher salt

Dash Angostura bitters

Ice cubes

Rub the lemon zest strip around the rim of a coupe, then add it to the glass. In a cocktail shaker, combine the gin, maraschino liqueur, Bénédictine, Lillet Blanc, salt and bitters. Shake with ice cubes. Strain into the glass.

POUR ME ANOTHER
★ NOW TRY ★

Air Mail, 197
Painkiller, 194

PEGU CLUB COCKTAIL

The Pegu Club Cocktail was created around the early 1900s at a Burmese social club of the same name, which itself was named for the nearby Pegu River. It's a variation of a Gimlet and features gin, lime juice, orange liqueur and bitters. The goal is a refreshing cocktail, but too often that is sacrificed to mouth-puckering sourness that overwhelms the nuances of the gin. In this version, we lose the lime juice in favor of a lime zest strip, which is rubbed around the rim of the glass before being added to it. A bit of dry vermouth brings clean herbal notes without added sweetness. The result is reminiscent of a light, bright, slightly citrusy and wonderfully creamy martini.

1 lime zest strip

2 ounces gin

½ ounce orange liqueur

½ ounce dry vermouth

⅛ ounce (¾ teaspoon) agave or
   simple syrup

Dash Angostura bitters

Dash orange bitters

6 to 10 granules kosher salt

Ice cubes

Rub the lime zest strip around the rim of a coupe, then add it to the glass. In a cocktail shaker, combine the gin, orange liqueur, dry vermouth, syrup, both bitters and the salt. Shake with ice cubes, then strain into the coupe.

POUR ME ANOTHER

★ NOW TRY ★

Parisian Blonde, 195
Coconut-Lime Daiquiri, 199
Lime in de Coconut, 83

TUXEDO

Harry Johnson codified this peppy take on the Gin Martini in the late 1800s in his *Bartenders' Manual*. It's a simple mix of gin and dry vermouth that gets complexity from a few dashes of absinthe and a hint of sweet from a few more of maraschino. Johnson's recipe calls for orange bitters. Later versions sometimes ditched the bitters in favor of lemon zest or—in the case of Dale DeGroff, who adopted Charles S. Mahoney's 1905 take on the Tuxedo in *Hoffman House Bartender's Guide*—replaced it with nothing at all. I find the floral-sweet orange bitters help balance the vermouth and absinthe.

1½ ounces gin

1 ounce dry vermouth

2 dashes absinthe

2 dashes maraschino liqueur

Dash orange bitters

Ice cubes

In a stirring glass, combine the gin, vermouth, absinthe, maraschino and bitters. Stir with ice cubes, then strain into a Nick and Nora glass or a coupe.

POUR ME ANOTHER
★ NOW TRY ★

Vodka Hurricane, 90

PINK LADY

The Pink Lady has been kicking around for at least 100 years, and depending on which recipe you use she's starting to show her age. In 1920, Harry MacElhone included a simple version in *Harry's ABC of Mixing Cocktails*—a basic shake of gin, brandy, grenadine and egg white. Ten years later, Harry Craddock pared her back, losing the brandy. But by 1948, when David Embury included the cocktail in *The Fine Art of Mixing Drinks,* the brandy wasn't just back, it had become apple brandy and it brought along some lemon juice. And both were there to stay. These changes gave it more than a passing resemblance to a White Lady, a cocktail of similar vintage that swaps orange liqueur for the brandy and simple syrup for the grenadine. Both live in the world of gin sours, a little too much so for my tastes.

For my version, I took my cue from Craddock and ditched the lemon juice (some recipes call for a full—and overwhelming— 1 ounce). To keep the citrus flavor without the acidity, I followed the lead of Charles H. Baker Jr., whose *The Gentleman's Companion* recounts a version he encountered at Miramar Club in Panama City during the '30s. It contained many changes, including the addition of orange bitters. Fruity still, but sour no more.

POUR ME ANOTHER
★ NOW TRY ★

Clover Club, 46
Coconut-Lime Daiquiri, 199

2 ounces gin
½ ounce egg white
½ ounce apple brandy

¼ ounce grenadine
Dash orange bitters
Ice cubes

In a cocktail shaker, combine the gin, egg white, brandy, grenadine and bitters. Dry shake without ice, then add ice and shake again. Strain into a coupe.

SINGAPORE SLING

The Singapore Sling is a fruity sugar bomb created—at least by most accounts—during the very early 1900s at the Long Bar at Raffles Hotel in Singapore. Many versions have proliferated since then, but most are some variation of a gin sling—some blend of gin, sugar, juice and bubbles. Except the juice and sugar too often dominate and you might as well just pop a can of fruit cocktail, add some bubblegum vodka and call it a day. My version refines this equation, getting a little pop from ginger liqueur and some peppery notes from rye (a common alternative to the gin, but I like to use both). Though this typically is a long drink, I cut it back to a coupe by limiting the bubbles to just a splash.

1 ounce gin

1 ounce rye

¾ ounce orange juice

¼ ounce ginger liqueur

¼ ounce agave or simple syrup

3 dashes Angostura bitters

Ice cubes

Splash sparkling wine

In a cocktail shaker, combine the gin, rye, orange juice, ginger liqueur, syrup and bitters. Shake with ice cubes. Strain into a coupe. Top with sparkling wine.

POUR ME ANOTHER

★ NOW TRY ★

Dark and Stormy, 187
Tropical Itch, 201
Fog Cutter, 188
Mai Tai, 189
Latin Love, 191

GIN PUNCH

Jerry Thomas, of 1862 *Bartender's Guide* fame, contends that a proper punch always begins by muddling lemon zest and sugar. For his Gin Punch, he then piles on the fruity flavors, starting with raspberry syrup, then moving on to orange slices, lemon juice and pineapple. I reined it in a bit, subbing raspberry jam for the syrup, which gives the finished cocktail a better mouthfeel. Orange and ginger liqueurs stand in for the fruit, sweetening the drink without overwhelming or diluting it. You can skip the celery bitters if you don't have them handy, but they bring a salty-savory quality that wonderfully balances everything. For a more intense fruity flavor, skip the agave and use 2 teaspoons raspberry jam.

1 lemon zest strip	¼ ounce lemon juice
1 teaspoon raspberry jam	¼ ounce agave or simple syrup
2½ ounces gin	Dash celery bitters
¼ ounce orange liqueur	6 to 10 granules kosher salt
¼ ounce ginger liqueur	Ice, cubes and crushed

In a cocktail shaker, muddle the lemon zest strip and the jam. Leave the muddler in the shaker. Add the gin, orange liqueur, ginger liqueur, lemon juice, syrup, bitters and salt. Swish the muddler to rinse it, then remove. Shake with ice cubes, then double strain into a coupe filled halfway with crushed ice.

POUR ME ANOTHER
★ NOW TRY ★
Between the Sheets, 185
French 75, 30
Bay Breeze, 80
Tiki Tundra, 81
Tropical Itch, 201
Army and Navy, 29
Opium, 236
Cancan, 85

ANGEL IN THE AIR

This cocktail is an update on the Blue Devil, which lives in the delicious space between two more storied classics—The Aviation and the Singapore Sling. The former too often is wildly sour and the latter is crazy sweet. The Blue Devil isn't much better. It gets its namesake color from blue Curaçao, an orange liqueur with blue food coloring. Thanks, but I'll pass. The Angel in the Air keeps the fruity sweetness we love in these cocktails, but dials back the juice while balancing everything with some bitters and salt. Some ginger liqueur fits right in, brightening everything without overwhelming.

1½ ounces gin

½ ounce maraschino liqueur

¼ ounce ginger liqueur

¼ ounce orange liqueur

¼ ounce lemon juice

Dash orange bitters

6 to 10 granules kosher salt

Ice cubes

In a cocktail shaker, combine the gin, maraschino liqueur, ginger liqueur, orange liqueur, lemon juice, bitters and salt. Shake with ice cubes, then strain into a coupe with 1 large ice cube.

POUR ME ANOTHER
★ NOW TRY ★

Sneaky Sleeper, 95

BENNETT

The classic Bennett—created about 100 years ago—is a simple spin on the Gimlet, a happy mix of gin, lime juice and a splash of sugar. The Bennett brings balance to that mix with the addition of Angostura bitters. That helps, but the Bennett still tends to be a sour bomb. For this version, we tamp down the lime juice—often mixed at a 1:2 ratio to gin—to just ¼ ounce to a robust 3 ounces of gin. That retains the bright, citrus notes of the lime juice without obliterating the nuances of the gin. The twist? A little dry vermouth, which adds herbal notes that complement both the gin and the lime juice.

3 ounces gin
½ ounce agave or simple syrup
½ ounce dry vermouth
¼ ounce lime juice

Dash Angostura bitters
6 to 10 granules kosher salt
Ice cubes

In a cocktail shaker, combine the gin, syrup, vermouth, lime juice, bitters and salt. Shake with ice cubes. Strain into a rocks glass with 1 large or 2 standard ice cubes.

POUR ME ANOTHER

★ NOW TRY ★

Roman Punch, 205
Sex on the Beach, 96
Navy Grog, 222
Knickerbocker, 206
Grandfather, 135
A Slice of Pie, 97
Mr. 404, 100

SATAN'S WHISKERS

FRUITY

SWEET

STRONG

The classic Satan's Whiskers is a bright, citrusy and often too sweet combination of gin, orange liqueur, dry vermouth, sweet vermouth, orange juice and orange bitters. It can drink like an overwrought Orange Martini. So let's slow that roll a bit. The gin, dry vermouth and orange liqueur play so well together, why muck it up with sweet vermouth? And don't even get me started on the orange juice. A strip of orange zest gets us all the bright, fresh flavor we need without muddying the flavors with juice.

1 orange zest strip
Ice, cubes and crushed
2 ounces gin
½ ounce dry vermouth
½ ounce orange liqueur

⅛ ounce (¾ teaspoon) agave
   or simple syrup
6 to 10 granules kosher salt
Dash orange bitters

Rub the orange zest strip around the rim of a coupe, then add it to the glass. Fill the glass halfway with crushed ice. In a cocktail shaker, combine the gin, vermouth, orange liqueur, syrup, salt and bitters. Shake with ice cubes, then strain into the coupe.

POUR ME ANOTHER
✴ NOW TRY ✴

Ginger Screw, 101
Roman Punch, 205
Improved Screwdriver, 98
A Slice of Pie, 97
Mr. 404, 100
Sex on the Beach, 96

CLOVER CLUB

FRUITY
SWEET
CREAMY
HERBAL

The Clover Club gets its name from a men's social club that met at Philadelphia's Bellevue-Stratford Hotel during the late 1800s. It's a creamy, fruity concoction made from gin, lemon juice (though older recipes as often called for lime), raspberry syrup, egg white and (sometimes) dry vermouth. Harry MacElhone's *Harry's ABC of Mixing Cocktails* notes that by 1920, London bars had been making the cocktail with grenadine rather than raspberry syrup. A couple years later, Robert Vermeire's *Cocktails: How to Mix Them* offered a variation called the Clover Leaf, which added some muddled mint to the mix. For my take on the Clover Club, I ditched the vermouth, as it tends to get lost under the other, brighter flavors. I stuck with lemon juice, which plays so nicely with raspberry (here provided by jam). I also kept London's twist of grenadine, which adds a bracing quality. The mint is optional, but lovely.

2½ ounces gin

¾ ounce egg white

1 large sprig (4 to 5 leaves) fresh mint, slapped (optional), plus 1 leaf to garnish

1 teaspoon raspberry jam

½ ounce grenadine

¼ ounce lemon juice

6 to 10 granules kosher salt

Ice cubes

In a cocktail shaker, combine the gin, egg white, mint (if using), jam, grenadine, lemon juice and salt. Shake with ice cubes, then double strain into a coupe. Top with a mint leaf.

POUR ME ANOTHER

★ NOW TRY ★

Pink Lady, 40
Sex on the Beach, 96
Fedora, 208
Knickerbocker, 206
Improved Screwdriver, 98
Grandfather, 135
A Slice of Pie, 97

SLOW SCREW
MISSIONARY STYLE

The Screwdriver cocktail is a wild rabbit hole to research. It started as a basic vodka-orange juice blend served tall with plenty of ice. But then the vodka was swapped out for sloe gin, creating a new cocktail called the Slow Screw (also called a Sloe Screw). That's all it took to birth numerous saucy iterations. Add Southern Comfort and you get the Slow Comfortable Screw. Add Galliano (a sweet Italian liqueur that is a key ingredient for a Harvey Wallbanger) and you get a Slow Comfortable Screw Up Against the Wall. Toss in some peach schnapps and you have a Slow Comfortable Screw Up Against a Fuzzy Wall. And the list goes on and on. So this is my contribution to the whole sordid affair. I attempt to balance the sweetness of the basic gin Slow Comfortable Screw with the pepperiness of rye (instead of Southern Comfort) and herbal Bénédictine.

Ice cubes

3 ounces orange juice

1 ounce gin

1 ounce rye

½ ounce Bénédictine

Dash Angostura bitters

In a highball glass filled halfway with ice cubes, stir the orange juice, gin, rye, Bénédictine and bitters.

POUR ME ANOTHER

★ NOW TRY ★

Ginger Screw, 101
Improved Screwdriver, 98
Harvey Wallbanger, 103
Mr. 404, 100

CORPSE REVIVER

The original Corpse Reviver—one of a large and long-lived family of drinks that supposedly pull one back from the abyss of a long night of drinking—has been around since at least the mid-1800s, when it was a potent, sweet concoction of equal parts brandy and maraschino liqueur cut by some bitters. Over time, many iterations were born, most notably the Corpse Reviver No. 2, a blend of gin, lemon juice, orange liqueur and a touch of absinthe (among other ingredients) mainstreamed by the American Bar at The Savoy hotel in London. My version keeps the gin and orange liqueur, but loses the lemon juice in favor of less acidic orange liqueur. White wine lightens the load a bit, though you could skip that and add extra gin. I use fennel seeds in place of the absinthe wash many people use on the glass. That anise flavor is key to tying all the other parts together.

¼ teaspoon fennel seeds	½ ounce orange liqueur
¼ ounce agave or simple syrup	Dash Angostura bitters
2 ounces gin	6 to 10 granules kosher salt
1 ounce dry white wine	Ice cubes

POUR ME ANOTHER

★ NOW TRY ★

Vodka Fix, 102

In a cocktail shaker, muddle the fennel seeds and syrup. Leave the muddler in the shaker, then add the gin, wine, orange liqueur, bitters and salt. Swish the muddler to rinse it, then remove. Shake with ice cubes. Double strain into a rocks glass with 2 standard ice cubes or 1 large.

OCEAN SHORE

In 1890, California mixologist William Boothby published one of the most comprehensive "pamphlets" of cocktail recipes to date—*Cocktail Boothby's American Bartender.* In time, this morphed into *The World's Drinks and How to Mix Them,* a rollicking exploration of the state of cocktails from its era. While many of the drinks no longer quite hold up, there are a few hidden gems in its pages, including the Ocean Shore. Boothby's recipe calls for gin cut with either raspberry or orgeat syrup and lemon juice, all of it tied together with creamy egg white.

Why pick between raspberries and orgeat, which are wonderful together? To keep the sweet under control, I use fresh raspberries muddled with orgeat. Lemon juice tended to put the sour notes over the top, but a lemon zest strip muddled with the raspberries was perfect. After many attempts, I did ditch the egg white, which made the drink cloyingly thick. You won't miss it. The result is sweet and creamy and a little fruity. This is an excellent starter cocktail for the person who thinks they don't like gin. The origins of the name? Your guess is as good as mine.

POUR ME ANOTHER

★ NOW TRY ★

Latin Love, 191
Mary Pickford Cocktail, 207
Spiced Orange Daiquiri, 193
Jungle Bird, 225
Toronjil, 241

2 raspberries	2½ ounces gin
¼ ounce orgeat syrup	Dash orange bitters
1 lemon zest strip	Ice cubes

In a cocktail shaker, combine the raspberries, orgeat and lemon zest strip. Aggressively muddle, then leave the muddler in the shaker. Add the gin and bitters, then swish the muddler to rinse it. Remove the muddler. Shake with ice cubes, then double strain into a Nick and Nora glass.

THE SWEET PATOOTIE

This 1920s cocktail is all about the orange, blending gin with orange juice and orange liqueur. The classic is called The Sweet Patootie, a term that once was slang for girlfriend. The original ratio was 2:1:1 gin to juice to liqueur. But to let the botanicals cut through the citrusy sweetness, I changed that to 4:1:1. I also added a splash of vanilla-spice Licor 43 because it plays so well with orange. A hint of salt balances the sweetness.

2 ounces gin

½ ounce orange liqueur

½ ounce orange juice

¼ ounce Licor 43

6 to 10 granules kosher salt

Ice cubes

In a cocktail shaker, combine the gin, orange liqueur, orange juice, Licor 43 and salt. Shake with ice cubes, then strain into a cocktail glass.

POUR ME ANOTHER
★ NOW TRY ★

Sex on the Beach, 96
Loud Speaker, 67
Orange Martini, 68

THE MONKEY GLAND

SWEET

FRUITY

SOUR

HERBAL

As the story goes, a Russian doctor believed that grafting a monkey testicle into a human somehow extended the person's life. And during the 1920s, that—somehow!?!—inspired the creation of The Monkey Gland cocktail, a sweetly licoricey blend of gin, orange juice, grenadine and absinthe. Unless made with the greatest of care, the drink can be unappealingly cloying and overwhelmed by anise. The latter I solve by muddling fennel seeds with just a splash of grenadine, a combination that delivers a finer hit of both sweet and anise. The Licor 43 rounds out everything with a gentle vanilla note.

¼ teaspoon fennel seeds

¼ ounce grenadine

3 ounces gin

½ ounce orange juice

¼ ounce Licor 43

Dash Angostura bitters

6 to 10 granules kosher salt

Ice cubes

In a cocktail shaker, muddle the fennel seeds with the grenadine. Leave the muddler in the shaker. Add the gin, orange juice, Licor 43, bitters and salt. Swish the muddler to rinse it, then remove. Shake with ice cubes, then double strain into a coupe.

POUR ME ANOTHER

★ NOW TRY ★

Vodka Fix, 102
Corpse Reviver, 48
Gin Daisy, 57
Paloma, 255
Navy Grog, 222

BEE'S KNEES

The Bee's Knees cocktail—a version of the basic Sour—dates to Prohibition, when heavy doses of lemon juice and honey were needed to mask the flavor of rotgut gin. We've come a long way. Now that we don't need to camouflage the booze, we can adjust the proportions to let the gin shine. This version backs down both the honey and lemon juice to ¼ ounce each. The addition of orange bitters keeps the citrus flavors high without additional acidity. The ginger liqueur adds a similar sharpness—the stinger, if you will.

¼ ounce honey
2½ ounces gin
¼ ounce lemon juice
¼ ounce ginger liqueur

Dash orange bitters
6 to 10 granules kosher salt
Ice, cubes and crushed

In a cocktail shaker, combine the honey, gin, lemon juice, ginger liqueur, bitters and salt. Shake with ice cubes. Strain into a rocks glass filled halfway with crushed ice.

POUR ME ANOTHER
★ NOW TRY ★

Navy Grog, 222
Vodka Caipirinha, 115
Cherry-Lime Vodka Rickey, 109
Vodka Gimlet, 118
Bay Breeze, 80
Sex on the Beach, 96
Cosmopolitan, 111

GIN RICKEY

SWEET

SOUR

CREAMY

The classic Gin Rickey is tall, icy, bubbly and sour. Most recipes today are little more than gin, way too much lime juice, sugar and club soda. But if you look back over its at least 150-year history, you see that there is plenty of room to play with that equation. I drew inspiration first from William Boothby's 1908 *The World's Drinks and How to Mix Them*. Rather than lime juice, he instead calls for muddling fresh lime into the drink. This contributes less juice and acidity, but more flavor to the finished cocktail (thanks to the essential oils released by the skin of the lime). This alone was a big improvement, but it still needed refinement. The lime tended to dominate the gin. So I kept Boothby's muddling approach, but used only a strip of lime zest. This delivers big citrus flavor minus the acidic juice. I also liked a forgotten variation lauded by David Embury, who dedicated three pages of *The Fine Art of Mixing Drinks* to the lore of the Rickey. Among his favorite variations? One spiked with apricot brandy. Finally, my own twist was to ditch the highball glass and keep this a short pour.

1 lime zest strip

¼ ounce agave or simple syrup

2½ ounces gin

¼ ounce apricot brandy

6 to 10 granules kosher salt

Ice cubes

Splash club soda

POUR ME ANOTHER

* NOW TRY *

Vodka Rickey, 109

In a cocktail shaker, aggressively muddle the zest strip and syrup. Leave the muddler in the shaker. Add the gin, brandy and salt, then swish the muddler to rinse it. Remove the muddler. Shake with ice cubes, then double strain into a Nick and Nora glass. Top with club soda.

SALTY DOG

The Salty Dog likely started life as the Greyhound during the 1930s, when Harry Craddock mixed grapefruit juice with gin. A few decades later, somebody added salt and the Salty Dog was born. It's a rare exception in cocktails, which generally lean sweet. The Salty Dog is supposed to taste a little briny, an interesting match to the botanicals of the gin and the sweet-sour grapefruit. Over the years, many bartenders decided to give the Salty Dog a margarita treatment, skipping the salt in the cocktail and instead adding it to the rim of the glass.

I'm a big believer in salting cocktails (see page 23). But I struggled to make a modern Salty Dog I enjoyed. No matter which version I tried, the grapefruit juice—used almost always in a 2:1 ratio to gin—overwhelmed the liquor, turning it bitter. At that point, the salt only made the mess worse.

The solution turned out to be obvious: Give the Salty Dog the real Margarita treatment—but not its salty rim. Take the flavor profile of the original, but use the proportions of a margarita. In place of the classic orange liqueur that rides shotgun to tequila, I took a tip from Dale DeGroff's Salty Dog Retooled, which, among other changes, adds elderflower liqueur (and bitters).

As for the salt? I stick with my usual approach. Too much salt—particularly on the rim of the glass—blows out the flavors of a cocktail. But just a hint rounds out and blooms the other flavors. That's the approach I took here. It produced a far better, far more balanced cocktail than the seawater approach of so many other recipes.

POUR ME ANOTHER

★ NOW TRY ★

Vodka Salty Dog, 116
Lemon Drop, 117

2 ounces gin

1 ounce grapefruit juice

¾ ounce elderflower liqueur

6 to 10 granules kosher salt

Dash Angostura bitters

Ice cubes

In a cocktail shaker, combine the gin, juice, elderflower liqueur, salt and bitters. Shake with ice cubes, then strain into a coupe.

INCA

Details are sketchy regarding the Inca cocktail, which has been around for at least 100 years. It appears in Robert Vermeire's 1922 *Cocktails: How to Mix Them,* where it is credited to H. C. Harrison, who preceded Vermeire at London's Embassy Club. It pops up in several other guides of the era, and in each case the formula is similar. Equal parts gin, dry sherry and dry vermouth tempered by a bit of orgeat syrup and orange bitters, and almost always finished with a chunk of pineapple.

1 ounce gin

1 ounce dry sherry

1 ounce dry vermouth

⅛ ounce (¾ teaspoon) orgeat syrup

Dash orange bitters

Ice cubes

Chunk fresh pineapple

In a cocktail shaker, combine the gin, sherry, vermouth, orgeat and bitters. Shake with ice cubes, then strain into a coupe and add the pineapple on a cocktail skewer.

POUR ME ANOTHER
★ NOW TRY ★

El Presidente Cocktail, 224
Vodka Special, 110
Loud Speaker, 67

DEATH IN THE GULFSTREAM

American journalist Charles H. Baker Jr. set out in 1931 to explore food and drink around the world. The results were two thick manuals: *The Gentleman's Companion Volume I: The Exotic Cookery Book* and *The Gentleman's Companion Volume II: Being an Exotic Drinking Book or, Around the World with Jigger, Beaker, and Flask*. That last one is packed with incomparable gems, including this cocktail supposedly gleaned from Ernest Hemingway while fishing and drinking away many a day. With refreshments such as this, it's hard to imagine much fishing occurred. Described as a collins glass filled with crushed ice, the juice of a lime, a few dashes of Angostura bitters and a tall pour of gin, the name kind of explains itself. Hemingway didn't allow for any sweetener, but Baker said "not more than 1 tsp" was permissible.

To keep this cocktail from truly killing us, I ditched the collins for a rocks glass, kept the crushed ice, then stirred the gin with a bit of lime, syrup and bitters. The result is refreshing, bright and sour. It matures wonderfully in the glass, drinking like a Margarita. Serve as a chaser to a hot, sunny day.

POUR ME ANOTHER

★ NOW TRY ★

Vodka Caipirinha, 115
Zombie, 231

3 ounces gin

¼ ounce lime juice

¼ ounce agave or simple syrup

4 dashes Angostura bitters

6 to 10 granules kosher salt

Crushed ice

1 lime round

In a stirring glass, combine the gin, lime juice, syrup, bitters and salt. Stir without ice. Pour into a rocks glass filled halfway with crushed ice. Add the lime round.

GIN DAISY

SOUR

SWEET

HERBAL

This citrusy gin cocktail has been around since at least 1882, when Harry Johnson included it in his *Bartenders' Manual*. His was a stirred blend of lemon and lime juices combined with sugar, seltzer water, gin and herbal-sweet Yellow Chartreuse. Over time, many versions dropped the Chartreuse, replacing it with grenadine and favoring just one of the juices. By 1948, David Embury had decided the grenadine and Chartreuse didn't need to be an either/or situation. I opted for his take on this, but retained Johnson's combination of lemon and lime.

2 ounces gin

½ ounce Yellow Chartreuse

¼ ounce grenadine

⅛ ounce (¾ teaspoon) lemon juice

⅛ ounce (¾ teaspoon) lime juice

Ice cubes

In a stirring glass, combine the gin, Chartreuse, grenadine and both juices. Stir with ice cubes, then strain into a cocktail glass.

POUR ME ANOTHER
★ NOW TRY ★

Vodka Fix, 102

BIJOU

The Bijou is from around 1890, when it was made with equal parts gin, sweet vermouth and Green Chartreuse. It's a combination that is reminiscent of a lighter, brighter Old Fashioned. But the original ratio could leave the Bijou feeling a bit rough at the edges. In recent decades the volume of gin crept up, an improvement credited to bartending legend Dale DeGroff. In this version, I nudge the Green Chartreuse down even more; it easily overwhelms and is best appreciated as a background note. I also add Angostura bitters to the more conventional orange bitters, which—combined with a tiny pinch of salt—results in a perfectly rounded, balanced cocktail.

2 ounces gin
1 ounce sweet vermouth
½ ounce Green Chartreuse
Dash Angostura bitters

Dash orange bitters
6 to 10 granules kosher salt
Ice cubes

In a stirring glass, combine the gin, vermouth, Green Chartreuse, both bitters and the salt. Stir with ice cubes. Strain into a coupe.

POUR ME ANOTHER
★ NOW TRY ★

Old Fashioned, 131
Manhattan, 153
Vieux Carré, 180

THE HORSE THIEF

This smooth, yet complex cocktail was created by Tom Bullock, the first Black bartender to publish a cocktail book. *The Ideal Bartender* was released in 1917 and its 173 recipes set the standard for decades to come. His Horse Thief was a stirred blend of absinthe, sweet vermouth and gin, a combination with depth and gentle sweetness. I find a hint of salt helps elevate and round out the anise notes of the absinthe and the fruity-herbal side of the vermouth.

2 ounces gin
½ ounce sweet vermouth
¼ ounce absinthe

6 to 10 granules kosher salt
Ice cubes

In a stirring glass, combine the gin, vermouth, absinthe and salt. Stir with ice cubes, then strain into a cocktail glass.

POUR ME ANOTHER
★ NOW TRY ★

Well-Spoken Russian, 121
Manhattan, 153
Vesper, 71

HANKY PANKY

This classy little sweet and strong number is a relative of The Horse Thief, with bitter Fernet-Branca amaro standing in for the absinthe. Credit for its creation in the early 1900s goes to Ada Coleman of American Bar at The Savoy hotel in London. She made it for a frequent customer fond of asking for a drink with "a bit of punch in it." Apparently, when the customer first tasted this cocktail, he responded with, "By Jove! That is the real hanky-panky!"

2 ounces gin

½ ounce sweet vermouth

⅛ ounce (¾ teaspoon)
   Fernet-Branca amaro

6 to 10 granules kosher salt

Ice cubes

Orange zest twist

In a stirring glass, combine the gin, vermouth, amaro and salt. Stir with ice cubes, then strain into a coupe. Garnish with the zest twist.

POUR ME ANOTHER
★ NOW TRY ★

Well-Spoken Russian, 121
Yellow Parrot, 125
The Horse Thief, 59

NEGRONI

BITTER
CREAMY
REFRESHING
FRUITY

The origins of the Negroni—a bittersweet blend of equal parts gin, Campari and sweet vermouth—are murky. Most say it was created in Florence, Italy, around 1919 when Count Camillo Negroni asked a bartender to sub gin for the soda water in his Americano cocktail. Others say a different Count Negroni concocted it in 1857 in Senegal. Regardless of which count gets the credit, a Negroni typically is garnished with an orange zest strip, its flavorful oils adding a citrusy note to this slow sipper. That seemed the right place to jump off for this lighter, brighter take on the classic. We skip the sweet vermouth in favor of a blend of equally sweet but more interesting (and floral and peppery) orange Curaçao (any orange liqueur can be substituted) and ginger liqueur. The result is pleasantly bitter, but also vivid, refreshing and just a bit creamy.

1½ ounces gin
½ ounce orange Curaçao
½ ounce ginger liqueur
½ ounce Campari

Dash orange bitters
6 to 10 granules kosher salt
Ice cubes

In a cocktail shaker, combine the gin, Curaçao, ginger liqueur, Campari, bitters and salt. Shake with ice cubes, then strain into a coupe with 1 large ice cube.

POUR ME ANOTHER
★ NOW TRY ★

Jungle Bird, 225
Boulevardier, 150
La Rosita, 275
The Red Devil, 257
Old Pal, 62
Amber on the Rocks, 87
Agave Spritz, 276

OLD PAL

BITTER
SWEET
FRUITY
SOUR

This cocktail has had more costume changes than Liberace. So let's trace it back to its roots as an offshoot of the Negroni, a lovely blend of gin, sweet vermouth and Campari. At some point, a clever mixologist swapped rye for the gin and created the Boulevardier, now a classic unto itself. Jump forward and somebody else swapped dry vermouth for the sweet vermouth, giving the world the Old Pal. Jim Meehan then took the Old Pal back (somewhat) to its origins, returning the core liquor to gin and ditching the vermouth entirely in favor of sweetly floral St-Germain elderflower liqueur. He also added a splash of grapefruit juice, which brings this cocktail into Gin Sour territory. And that was my starting point. I kept much of his formula, but opted for Aperol over Campari because its more gentle bitter notes play better with the gin.

2 ounces gin	6 to 10 granules kosher salt
½ ounce Aperol	Ice cubes
½ ounce grapefruit juice	Lemon zest twist
¼ ounce elderflower liqueur	

In a cocktail shaker, combine the gin, Aperol, grapefruit juice, elderflower liqueur and salt. Shake with ice cubes, then strain into a coupe and garnish with the twist.

POUR ME ANOTHER

★ NOW TRY ★

Naked and Famous, 264
Angel's Share, 177
Agave Spritz, 276
Hemingway Daiquiri No. 2, 28

GIN AND IT

The Gin and It—a simple blend of gin, sweet vermouth and bitters—is rumored to be Queen Elizabeth's go-to cocktail. It's a relative of the Gin Manhattan, which calls for a similar formula but uses Angostura bitters where the Gin and It opts for orange bitters. The Gin Manhattan also typically tosses in a maraschino cherry. It's hard to argue with such delicious simplicity, so I simply tinkered with the proportions to make sure the gin isn't lost in the mix. For me, the spice of Angostura bitters won out, but we keep the clear, bright flavors of orange thanks to a strip of zest. The cherry was a keeper.

1 orange zest strip

2 ounces gin

1 ounce sweet vermouth

Dash Angostura bitters

Ice cubes

1 maraschino cherry

Rub the zest strip around the rim of a rocks glass, then add it to the glass. In a stirring glass, combine the gin, sweet vermouth and bitters. Stir with ice cubes, then strain into the glass. Add the cherry.

POUR ME ANOTHER
★ NOW TRY ★

Brave Bull, 265

THE DIRTY ORANGE

The origins of this one are blurred, but most evidence leads to Japan, where gin and local whiskey frequently are combined to great effect. Somewhere along the line, the folks at Sipsmith in London decided the whiskey should be replaced by Kahlúa—they call it the Chiswick in Black. It seems odd, until you taste it. Creamy, chocolatey and spicy, yet not heavy. I added orange liqueur and bitters, because orange and chocolate love each other so very much.

2 ounces gin

1 ounce Kahlúa

½ ounce orange liqueur

6 to 10 granules kosher salt

Dash orange bitters

Ice cubes

In a cocktail shaker, combine the gin, Kahlúa, orange liqueur, salt and bitters. Shake with ice cubes. Strain into a coupe.

POUR ME ANOTHER
★ NOW TRY ★

Orange Bat, 184
White(-ish) Russian, 88
Brando Russian, 91

THE MULE'S HIND LEG

This Prohibition-era cocktail's name presumably is a reference to the kick in the head this potent libation delivers. Classic versions—as told by Harry Craddock in *The Savoy Cocktail Book*—call for equal parts gin, Bénédictine, apple brandy, apricot brandy and maple syrup, shaken and strained. I found that all a bit much, leaning too hard into sweetness. I cleaned it up a bit, trimming out some sweetness to let the gin and Bénédictine take center stage, accented by the maple syrup and gentler cognac.

2 ounces gin
½ ounce Bénédictine
½ ounce cognac

⅛ ounce (¾ teaspoon) maple
syrup
Ice cubes

In a cocktail shaker, combine the gin, Bénédictine, cognac and maple syrup. Shake with ice cubes, then strain into a rocks glass.

POUR ME ANOTHER
★ NOW TRY ★

Gin Sling, 66
Ko Adang, 213
Rum Old Fashioned, 229
Aztec's Mark, 154

GIN SLING

Some variation of the Gin Sling has been around about as long as gin. Many early versions were merely gin, sugar and a finishing flourish of grated nutmeg. A cousin drink, the Gin Cocktail, loses the sugar in favor of a generous hand with orange bitters. My version combines the best of both. The orange and floral nutmeg work perfectly together, somehow creating an almost creamy flavor. I then double down on that creaminess with a hit of Licor 43 in place of the usual sugar. It adds a gentle spicy-vanilla sweetness that rounds everything perfectly. For best flavor and aroma, use whole nutmeg and grate it over the finished cocktail just before serving.

3 ounces gin

½ ounce Licor 43

Generous dash orange bitters

6 to 10 granules kosher salt

Ice, cubes and crushed

Pinch grated nutmeg

In a cocktail shaker, combine the gin, Licor 43, orange bitters and salt. Shake with ice cubes, then strain into a coupe filled halfway with crushed ice. Top with grated nutmeg.

POUR ME ANOTHER

★ NOW TRY ★

The Mule's Hind Leg, 65
Ko Adang, 213
Aztec's Mark, 154

LOUD SPEAKER

The classic Loud Speaker goes back to at least Harry Craddock's days at The Savoy hotel, where he describes this drink of equal parts brandy and gin as what "gives to radio announcers their peculiar enunciation." He adds that three of these cocktails pushes them to oscillation, and five triggers osculation (kissing). While certainly game to find out, I wanted this drink to be a bit more gin forward, as it can be lost behind the brandy (as well as the customary dashes of lemon juice and orange liqueur). I also found a sprinkle of salt and a bare hint of sugar helped round out the flavors, delivering a fuller, more balanced cocktail.

2 ounces gin

¾ ounce brandy

¼ ounce orange liqueur

⅛ ounce (¾ teaspoon)
   lemon juice

⅛ ounce (¾ teaspoon)
   agave or simple syrup

6 to 10 granules kosher salt

Ice cubes

In a cocktail shaker, combine the gin, brandy, orange liqueur, lemon juice, syrup and salt. Shake with ice cubes, then strain into a coupe.

POUR ME ANOTHER

★ NOW TRY ★

Pendennis Club, 69
Nutcracker, 132
Dandy, 156
Blood and Sand, 157
Orange Martini, 68
Linstead Cocktail, 159

ORANGE MARTINI

STRONG
FRUITY

If you go searching for Orange Martini recipes, brace yourself for a sugary onslaught. The internet is littered with juicy concoctions, often made with flavored vodkas and coconut rums. But take a turn back almost 100 years and you get something far more sophisticated and satisfying. Harry Craddock spells out a simple infused martini that blends gin, dry vermouth and sweet vermouth infused for two hours with orange zest. The mixture then is strained and added to a glass rinsed with orange bitters.

While I appreciate the simplicity of this approach, I prefer not to wait two hours to have a drink. I find that muddling the orange zest with the dry vermouth produces just as good an infusion. The original version rinsed the inside of the serving glass with orange bitters, but I found the flavor better to simply add them to the cocktail itself. The result is a martini that is pleasantly dry, yet brightly fruity.

Three 2-inch strips orange zest	Dash orange bitters
½ ounce dry vermouth	6 to 10 granules kosher salt
2 ounces gin	Ice cubes
½ ounce sweet vermouth	

In a stirring glass, combine 2 of the zest strips and the dry vermouth. Aggressively muddle the zest. Add the gin, sweet vermouth, bitters and salt. Stir with ice cubes, then strain into a coupe. Float the remaining zest strip in the glass.

POUR ME ANOTHER

★ NOW TRY ★

Pendennis Club, 69
Vodka Old Fashioned, 124
Nutcracker, 132
Dandy, 156
Blood and Sand, 157
The Sweet Patootie, 50

PENDENNIS CLUB

Named for the Kentucky social club where the cocktail supposedly originated 100 years or so ago, the Pendennis Club is a gentle Gin Sour that gets its sweetness—as well as pleasant fruitiness—from apricot brandy. Gin, lime juice and Peychaud's bitters round out most versions of the cocktail. But in *The Gentleman's Companion,* Charles H. Baker Jr. notes that the Pendennis Club actually is just a sweeter take on the Grande Bretagne Cocktail No. 1, which he considered "one of the five or six chief cocktails of the whole wide world." He was introduced to the Grande Bretagne in Athens—the drink takes its name from a luxury hotel there—where an Eddie Hastings introduced him to the whirlwind bartender who first concocted this. The main difference between the Pendennis Club and the Grande Bretagne Cocktail No. 1 is swapping orange bitters for the Peychaud's and the addition of an egg white.

I don't care for either typical version. But when I dug deeper, I discovered a pared-down Pendennis Club in the pages of William Boothby's 1907 *The World's Drinks and How to Mix Them.* His version ditches everything but the gin and apricot brandy and adds a splash of dry vermouth. That's the sort of delicious minimalism I can get behind—allowing the gin and apricot brandy to shine. In a nod to the usual lime, I rub the rim with a strip of zest.

POUR ME ANOTHER
★ NOW TRY ★

Loud Speaker, 67
Orange Martini, 68
Dandy, 156

Lime zest strip

1½ ounces gin

¾ ounce apricot brandy

¾ ounce dry vermouth

Ice cubes

Rub the zest strip around the rim of a coupe, then discard the zest. In a cocktail shaker, combine the gin, brandy and vermouth. Shake with ice cubes, then strain into the glass.

EXPOSITION COCKTAIL

This amber wonder is a deliciously smooth sipper whose origins are at least partly lost to time. William Boothby credited this cocktail to a mysterious Frank Doran in the 1908 edition of his *The World's Drinks and How to Mix Them*. His version called for equal parts gin, dry vermouth and cherry brandy. I downgraded the cherry brandy by half. Perhaps the options Doran and Boothby had back in the day were better than what is available to most of us now, but most brands today taste rather medicinal. That said, I was pleasantly surprised by the finished result of this cocktail. In fact, it shocked me by landing solidly as one of my favorites in the chapter for its clean, bright and only lightly fruity flavor.

1 ounce gin   **6 to 10 granules kosher salt**
1 ounce dry vermouth   **Ice cubes**
½ ounce cherry brandy

In a cocktail shaker, combine the gin, vermouth, brandy and salt. Shake with ice cubes, then strain into a cocktail glass.

POUR ME ANOTHER
★ NOW TRY ★

Dolce Vita, 133
Vesper, 71
Fish House Punch, 216
Oh, Henry! Cocktail, 162
Bull and Bear, 161

VESPER

As cocktails go, the Vesper is relatively young. It first appeared in Ian Fleming's 1953 James Bond novel, *Casino Royale*. The dashing spy initially orders a dry martini, then changes his mind and asks the bartender to make an unnamed cocktail from three parts gin, one part vodka and half that Kina Lillet (a fortified wine), shaken and finished with a lemon zest strip. Later in the book, the concoction gets its name from a double agent Bond is bedding, Vesper Lynd. But the drink itself actually was created for Fleming by a childhood friend, Ivar Bryce. Kina Lillet no longer is made, but it is similar to Lillet Blanc, though the latter lacks bitter quinine, which defined Kina Lillet. Both are fruity and lightly sweet. When making a Vesper, most people opt for Lillet Blanc, but in *Schofield's Fine and Classic Cocktails,* Joe and Daniel Schofield instead opt for Cocchi Americano, another fortified wine that has a similar flavor profile, but does include quinine. For my version, I followed their lead. The result is a strong, yet lightly fruity martini that allows the botanicals of the gin to shine. My contribution to this well-trod classic? The salt. It seems like a small thing, but just a few granules allow the fruit of the Cocchi Americano to stand up to and balance the gin.

POUR ME ANOTHER

★ NOW TRY ★

Exposition Cocktail, 70
Dolce Vita, 133
Fish House Punch, 216
Oh, Henry! Cocktail, 162
Bull and Bear, 161

3 ounces gin	6 to 10 granules kosher salt
1 ounce Cocchi Americano	Ice cubes
½ ounce vodka	Lemon zest twist

In a cocktail shaker, combine the gin, Cocchi Americano, vodka and salt. Shake with ice cubes, then strain into a cocktail glass. Garnish with the lemon twist.

THE LAST WORD

Cocktails built from equal parts of their various ingredients rarely work. The volumes may be balanced, but the flavors almost never are. The classic The Last Word is no exception. The original dates to around Prohibition at the Detroit Athletic Club and was made with equal parts gin, Green Chartreuse, maraschino liqueur and lime juice. It's a sweet-and-sour bomb in your mouth. My version upends those ratios in favor of more gin for more nuanced flavor. The addition of a bit of vanilla-forward Licor 43 rounds it out.

2½ ounces gin

½ ounce Green Chartreuse

½ ounce maraschino liqueur

¼ ounce Licor 43

Dash Angostura bitters

6 to 10 granules kosher salt

Ice cubes

In a cocktail shaker, combine the gin, Green Chartreuse, maraschino liqueur, Licor 43, bitters and salt. Shake with ice cubes, then strain into a coupe.

POUR ME ANOTHER
★ NOW TRY ★
Well-Spoken Russian, 121
La Ultima Palabra, 256
1920 Pick-Me-Up, 73
Martinez, 74
Make Your Mark, 76
Yellow Parrot, 125
De La Louisiane, 169
Remember the Maine, 144
Narragansett, 146

1920 PICK-ME-UP

STRONG
HERBAL
FRUITY
SWEET

This forgotten cocktail particularly deserves a renaissance. It's presumably named for the year Prohibition began, a year I'm guessing many a drinker needed a pick-me-up. I love how the gin is enhanced—but not overwhelmed—by the barest hints of absinthe and bitters. The result is impressively smooth and simple. The classic recipe finished the drink with soda, but I prefer to leave that out. Gum syrup—a cocktail sweetener made with sugar syrup and gum arabic, a thickener—is traditional and adds a faint viscosity, but simple syrup or agave are fine substitutes.

3 ounces gin

⅛ ounce (¾ teaspoon) absinthe

⅛ ounce (¾ teaspoon) gum or simple syrup

Dash Angostura bitters

Dash orange bitters

Ice cubes

In a cocktail shaker, combine the gin, absinthe, syrup and both bitters. Shake with ice cubes, then strain into a Nick and Nora glass.

POUR ME ANOTHER

★ NOW TRY ★

The Last Word, 72

Well-Spoken Russian, 121

La Ultima Palabra, 256

Martinez, 74

Make Your Mark, 76

Yellow Parrot, 125

De La Louisiane, 169

Remember the Maine, 144

Narragansett, 146

MARTINEZ

The Martinez dates to at least the mid-1800s. O. H. Byron's 1884 *The Modern Bartenders' Guide* described it as a Manhattan in which gin is substituted for the whiskey. Truth is, it's a bit more complicated than that. Robert Vermeire's 1922 *Cocktails: How to Mix Them* makes the same comparison, but his Manhattan calls for Curaçao and a dash of absinthe along with the rye and sweet vermouth. Harry Craddock of London's Savoy hotel followed the same model for his Martinez (though he ditched the absinthe and suggested maraschino as an optional alternative to the Curaçao). Boker's bitters (a variety of bitters that dates to 1828 and sports strong chocolate, cassia and cardamom notes) are traditional, but others use orange or Angostura or both. I wanted a version that is clean and allows the sweet and herbal notes to play with the botanicals of the gin. I kept the sweet vermouth and opted for orange liqueur over the now more common maraschino, but in a nod to the Manhattan, I finish it with a maraschino cherry. While Angostura bitters get the job done, go for more herbal Boker's if you have them.

POUR ME ANOTHER

★ NOW TRY ★

The Last Word, 72
Well-Spoken Russian, 121
1920 Pick-Me-Up, 73
La Ultima Palabra, 256

1½ ounces gin
1½ ounces sweet vermouth
¼ ounce orange liqueur
Dash Boker's or Angostura
  bitters

Ice cubes
1 maraschino cherry

In a stirring glass, combine the gin, sweet vermouth, orange liqueur and bitters. Stir with ice cubes. Strain into a coupe. Add the cherry.

GIN MARTINI

POUR ME ANOTHER

★ NOW TRY ★

The Last Word, 72
Well-Spoken Russian, 121
1920 Pick-Me-Up, 73
Martinez, 74
La Ultima Palabra, 256

During the early years of the Gin Martini—which was born around the late 1800s—it was cowboy country. Anything went. It might be shaken or stirred. It might be "dry" (dry vermouth and gin, nothing more), "medium" (a blend of sweet and dry vermouths) or "sweet" (sweet vermouth only). It also could have an orange twist instead of the now standard lemon (and then sometimes was called a Rosington or Roselyn, depending on which part of the U.S. you were in). Green olives were a common garnish. Orange bitters also were (and remain) a frequent flyer. Sifting and tasting my way through the history, I found myself gravitating back to basics. A simple stir of gin, dry vermouth and orange bitters—which add a gentle sweetness to the herbaceous botanicals. A generous ¾ ounce of dry vermouth keeps this version on the wetter side.

Before we drink, a note about getting dirty. A so-called dirty martini generally involves a splash of the brine from a jar of green olives. I find that even a conservative splash tends to overwhelm the other flavors, particularly if you aren't using premium olives. Rather, I prefer a trick from bartending brothers Joe and Daniel Schofield, who ditch the brine and instead muddle a few olives in the stirring glass, stir in the other ingredients, then strain out the olives. It adds wonderfully nuanced savory flavors that round out the other ingredients without going overboard. But feel free to skip the olive if you prefer your cocktail on the clean side. Finally, this is a long stir. Don't skimp: A full 10 seconds is needed to properly chill this cocktail.

1 green olive (such as
   Castelvetrano)
2 ounces gin
¾ ounce dry vermouth

Dash orange bitters
6 to 10 granules kosher salt
Ice cubes

In a stirring glass, gently muddle the olive. Add the gin, dry vermouth and bitters. Stir for 10 seconds with ice. Double strain into a coupe or cocktail glass.

MAKE YOUR MARK

STRONG

HERBAL

BITTER

SWEET

Take your basic Gin and It or Gin Manhattan, then toss in a bit of bourbon. Suddenly, you're straddling a delicious line that leans Old Fashioned. It's the brainchild of the folks at Sipsmith London (a lovely distillery) and Pryce Greenow of liquor behemoth Beam Suntory. Christened the Marksmith, the cocktail of equal parts gin, Maker's Mark bourbon and sweet vermouth is pleasantly stronger than your typical gin cocktail, in all the right ways. Taking it back to its Gin and It origins by reintroducing bitters gives it balance. And upping the gin a bit ensures the botanicals don't get lost beneath all that oak and sweetness.

Orange zest strip

1½ ounces gin

1 ounce bourbon

½ ounce sweet vermouth

¼ ounce agave or simple syrup

Dash Angostura bitters

Ice cubes

Rub the orange zest strip around the rim of a coupe, then add it to the glass. In a stirring glass, combine the gin, bourbon, sweet vermouth, syrup and bitters. Stir with ice cubes. Strain into the coupe.

POUR ME ANOTHER

★ NOW TRY ★

The Last Word, 72
Well-Spoken Russian, 121
1920 Pick-Me-Up, 73
La Ultima Palabra, 256

VODKA

Vodka's superpower is its ability to be anything for anyone. But mastery of vodka mixology isn't a matter of covering up the star ingredient. It's about accenting it and letting it steer the ship rather than be a bit player on the back deck. We start our exploration with the basic VODKA MARTINI, where a minimalist hand keeps the focus on how HERBAL dry vermouth dances with rather than dominates the vodka. If that's not your style, add a bit of lime juice for a VODKA GIMLET, which straddles the Margarita line. The VODKA SPECIAL adds maraschino liqueur to that mix for a fruitier take. Or if you're the SPICY sort, add some ginger for a MOSCOW MULE. And SOUR grapefruit juice and BITTER Aperol transform it into a VODKA SALTY DOG.

As with most liquors purchased for mixing, stick with the middle shelf when shopping. The nuance of premium bottles is lost in most cocktails. I'm happy with Tito's Handmade Vodka. And for the love of god, avoid flavored vodkas.

VODKA MARTINI

As with so many classics, origin stories for the Vodka Martini are difficult to parse. But it likely dates to the late 1880s, and began life as a blend of gin and sweet vermouth. It would take several decades before dry vermouth became widely available enough to edge its way into the Martini. And it wasn't until the 1960s that vodka stood on equal footing as gin.

Beyond that, there are a couple issues one must resolve when contemplating any martini. First, to shake or to stir? I side with Robert Simonson, author of *The Martini Cocktail,* who favors stirring martinis because it better preserves the visual clarity of the finished drink. Second, the dirt. A reference, of course, to the olive brine often added to a martini. Here, I strongly advocate for a bit of dirt. This is because just as in our food, in our cocktails a hint of salt heightens and brightens all the other flavors. And when those flavors are so clean and simple, as in a Vodka Martini, that salt is essential. The trick, of course, is to add just enough to enhance those flavor notes without adding a briny flavor able to be distinguished on its own. For this, I like to let the olives do the talking. Two green olives, speared on a cocktail skewer and dunked in the jar brine before being used to stir the finished cocktail in the glass are perfect. And finally, while I often am happy with mid-shelf bottles for most mixing, this is a case where you really ought to opt for the best bottles you can afford. Once again, with so few—and such clean, clear—ingredients, quality comes through.

POUR ME ANOTHER
★ NOW TRY ★

Gin Martini, 75
French Martini, 104
Vodka Old Fashioned, 124
Cancan, 85
Tuxedo, 39
Choker Cocktail, 148

3 ounces premium vodka	Ice cubes
½ ounce dry vermouth	2 green olives

In a stirring glass, combine the vodka and dry vermouth. Stir with ice cubes, then strain into a cocktail glass. Spear the olives on a cocktail skewer, then use them to gently stir the drink in the glass.

BAY BREEZE

Conventional wisdom holds that this simple and refreshing summer cocktail was the brainchild of Ocean Spray and the Cranberry Growers Association, who about 60 years ago didn't know what to do with their berries and decided to start crafting cocktails using the juice. It worked. The Bay Breeze is a relative of the Sea Breeze, which uses grapefruit juice instead of pineapple.

3 ounces vodka	Dash Angostura bitters
3 ounces sweetened cranberry juice	6 to 10 granules kosher salt
	Ice cubes
3 ounces pineapple juice	1 lime wedge

In a cocktail shaker, combine the vodka, cranberry juice and pineapple juice. Add the bitters and salt. Shake with ice cubes, then strain into a highball filled halfway with ice. Squeeze the lime wedge over the drink, then add it to the glass.

POUR ME ANOTHER
★ NOW TRY ★
Cosmopolitan, 111
Between the Sheets, 185
French 75, 30
Army and Navy, 29
Tiki Tundra, 81
Opium, 236

TIKI TUNDRA

This is the tiki drink for folks who don't care for rum. It's packed with fruity, refreshing goodness, and the clean flavor of the vodka allows you to keep your focus on that. Feel free to mix up the juices if you're so inclined. Mango, peach or guava can stand in for any of those called for. The Licor 43 is unusual for a tiki drink, but it adds wonderful sweet vanilla-spice flavors. If you don't have any, just up the vodka by another ½ ounce.

2 ounces vodka

1 ounce coconut water

½ ounce orange liqueur

½ ounce lime juice

½ ounce orange juice

½ ounce pineapple juice

½ ounce orgeat syrup

½ ounce Licor 43

Dash Angostura bitters

6 to 10 granules kosher salt

Ice, cubes and crushed

1 sprig fresh mint

In a cocktail shaker, combine the vodka, coconut water, orange liqueur, lime juice, orange juice, pineapple juice, orgeat syrup, Licor 43, bitters and salt. Shake with ice cubes, then strain into a highball filled halfway with crushed ice. Garnish with the mint.

POUR ME ANOTHER
★ NOW TRY ★

Between the Sheets, 185
Bay Breeze, 80
A Day at the Beach, 204
Cosmopolitan, 111

COSSACK

REFRESHING

SWEET

FRUITY

Named for the East Slavic Orthodox Christians who formed self-governing martial societies dating to the 15th century and today retain police-like roles in Russia, the Cossack is a potent yet bright blend of vodka, cognac, lime juice and sugar. Some versions use simple syrup, others use gomme, also called gum syrup, a sweetener that adds viscosity to the cocktail. If you have it, use it. Otherwise, agave or simple syrup will get the job done.

1½ ounces vodka

1½ ounces cognac

¼ ounce lime juice

¼ ounce gum or agave or simple syrup

Ice cubes

In a cocktail shaker, combine the vodka, cognac, lime juice and syrup. Shake with ice cubes, then strain into a coupe.

POUR ME ANOTHER

★ NOW TRY ★

The Derby, 140
Crimean Cup à La Marmora, 221
Gloom Chaser, 220
Boozy Smoothie, 107
All Jammed Up, 108
Lemon Drop, 117
The Big Apple, 139

LIME IN
DE COCONUT

This is my take on Dale DeGroff's lime- and coconut-heavy summer sipper that is light, refreshing and probably goes down a little too smooth. Where DeGroff uses ginger syrup, I opt for ginger liqueur. He calls for both coconut water and cream of coconut, but I find just the former adds plenty of tropical flavor and keeps the cocktail from tasting heavy.

2 lime rounds

¼ ounce agave or simple syrup

6 to 10 granules kosher salt

2½ ounces vodka

1 ounce coconut water

½ ounce ginger liqueur

Ice, cubes and crushed

In a cocktail shaker, muddle 1 lime round, the syrup and salt. Add the vodka, coconut water and ginger liqueur. Shake with ice cubes, then strain into a coupe or old fashioned glass filled halfway with crushed ice. Garnish with the second lime round.

POUR ME ANOTHER
★ NOW TRY ★

Coconut-Lime Daiquiri, 199
Gin and Tonic, 27
The Rum and the Restless, 190
Daiquiri, 183

BLOODY MARY

You could spend a lifetime trying to make sense of who first created the Bloody Mary. But regardless of whose tall tale you believe, most put its origins around the 1920s or '30s. The one consistent theme is the simplicity of the original—half vodka and half tomato juice, almost always served tall and over ice. From those simple beginnings, it has become one of the most bastardized cocktails. And don't even get me started about the ridiculous "garnishes" that adorn the more offensive versions, everything from strips of bacon to hunks of fried chicken and whole hamburgers. It's all a bit much. No surprise, I am not a fan of most modern Bloody Marys—so I pare it back to its origins. The result is a lovely and refreshing blend of vodka and vegetable juice (use just tomato, if you must) spiked with lemon, savory soy sauce, a hint of sugar and a bit of coconut water. That last element is unusual, but adds wonderfully light, tropical notes.

4 ounces vegetable juice
  (such as V8)
3 ounces vodka
2 ounces coconut water
½ ounce lemon juice
⅛ teaspoon soy sauce

⅛ teaspoon agave or simple
  syrup
6 to 12 generous dashes Tabasco
4 ice cubes
2 green olives, on a cocktail
  skewer

POUR ME ANOTHER

★ NOW TRY ★

El Vampiro, 259

In a stirring glass, combine the vegetable juice, vodka, coconut water, lemon juice, soy sauce, syrup, Tabasco and ice cubes. Stir, then strain into a highball. Garnish with the olives.

CANCAN

The Cancan is vodka's entry in the race to find the best French 75. There are plenty of cocktails that go under this name, but the version we are talking about follows roughly the same equation as the classic French 75—vodka, rather than gin, spiked with sparkling wine and a strip of lemon zest. Some versions ditch the sparkling wine in favor of elderflower liqueur and dry vermouth. Lovely, but not quite the same. For my Cancan, I stick closer to the original, adding a hint of sugar and Angostura bitters for balance.

2 ounces vodka

⅛ ounce (¾ teaspoon) agave or
   simple syrup

Dash Angostura bitters

2-inch lemon zest strip

Ice cubes

2 ounces sparkling wine

In a rocks glass, combine the vodka, syrup, bitters and lemon zest. Stir gently with 1 large or 2 standard ice cubes, then top with the sparkling wine.

POUR ME ANOTHER

★ NOW TRY ★

French 75, 30
Army and Navy, 29
Bay Breeze, 80
Tiki Tundra, 81
Between the Sheets, 185
Opium, 236

KRETCHMA

The classic Kretchma—apparently named for a spoof Russian drinking song—combines vodka, crème de cacao and grenadine with lemon juice. It's an unusual but pleasant combination. Still, since orange and chocolate are such fine bedfellows, I couldn't resist tinkering with David Embury's version of the drink by substituting orange juice for the lemon. The result is shockingly good—creamy, lightly fruity and just a hint sweet.

2 ounces vodka
½ ounce crème de cacao
½ ounce orange juice
¼ ounce grenadine
Ice cubes

In a cocktail shaker, combine the vodka, crème de cacao, orange juice and grenadine. Shake with ice cubes, then strain into a cocktail glass.

POUR ME ANOTHER
∗ NOW TRY ∗

Spiced Orange Daiquiri, 193
Creamsicle, 105
Jungle Bird, 225

AMBER
ON THE ROCKS

Bitter Aperol and creamy Licor 43 may not seem like great partners, but they play together perfectly. The result is creamy, sweet and just gently bitter. The vodka helps diffuse the sweetness without diluting the cocktail itself; the drink otherwise would be cloying.

2 ounces vodka

1 ounce Aperol

¼ ounce Licor 43

¼ ounce agave or simple syrup

6 to 10 granules kosher salt

Ice, cubes and crushed

In a cocktail shaker, combine the vodka, Aperol, Licor 43, syrup and salt. Shake with ice cubes, then strain into a coupe filled halfway with crushed ice.

POUR ME ANOTHER
⋆ NOW TRY ⋆

Parisian Blonde, 195
Buttered Rum, 196
Italian Margarita, 242
Air Mail, 197
A Day at the Beach, 204
White(-ish) Russian, 88
Guadalajara, 243
Painkiller, 194

WHITE(-ISH) RUSSIAN

The trouble with the classic White Russian is, well, the white part. Traditionally, heavy cream is at play, though sometimes milk or half-and-half is used. Vodka and coffee liqueur are combined in a rocks glass, then cream is poured over. Drinking the liquors through the layer of cream is supposed to be pleasant; I find it cloying. For my fix, I take the drink back closer to its roots—the Black Russian, which is simply vodka and coffee liqueur. I add creaminess to that base using unsweetened coconut water, rather than dairy. The result is more refreshing than you'd expect from a coffee cocktail, and far lighter.

2 ounces vodka
1½ ounces coconut water
1 ounce Kahlúa

6 to 10 granules kosher salt
Ice cubes

In a cocktail shaker, combine the vodka, coconut water, Kahlúa and salt. Shake with ice cubes, then strain into a Nick and Nora glass.

POUR ME ANOTHER
★ NOW TRY ★

Frangelic Beauty, 106
Brando Russian, 91

GYPSY QUEEN

In the Gypsy Queen, the wonderful herbal sweetness of Bénédictine shines through. The recipe supposedly goes back to the 1930s at New York City's Russian Tea Room. The original calls for orange bitters, but most versions today call for Angostura, which play better with the Bénédictine. The hint of salt also helps elevate all the other flavors, a key factor when there are so few prominent ingredients.

2 ounces vodka

¾ ounce Bénédictine

Dash Angostura bitters

6 to 10 granules kosher salt

Ice cubes

In a cocktail shaker, combine the vodka, Bénédictine, bitters and salt. Shake with ice cubes, then strain into Nick and Nora glass.

POUR ME ANOTHER

★ NOW TRY ★

The Mule's Hind Leg, 65
Gin Sling, 66
Ko Adang, 213
Rum Old Fashioned, 229
Aztec's Mark, 154

VODKA HURRICANE

CREAMY

HERBAL

STRONG

When people hear Hurricane, they think of the fruity, boozy rum drink from the tiki scene. But in 1948, David Embury wrote about another Hurricane, this one a simpler blend of vodka, cognac and absinthe. The result is strong, herbal and a little sweet—a sipper that shows off the deeper, darker side of vodka, yet remains oddly smooth. A testament to the power of herbal liqueurs to heighten and brighten.

2½ ounces vodka

½ ounce cognac

⅛ ounce (¾ teaspoon) absinthe

⅛ ounce (¾ teaspoon) agave or
   simple syrup

6 to 10 granules kosher salt

Ice cubes

In a cocktail shaker, combine the vodka, cognac, absinthe, syrup and salt. Shake with ice cubes, then strain into a Nick and Nora glass.

POUR ME ANOTHER
★ NOW TRY ★

Tuxedo, 39
Old George Sour, 244
Whiskey Sour, 163
Pink Lady, 40

BRANDO RUSSIAN

CREAMY

STRONG

SWEET

Supposedly created in Belgium by barman Gustave Tops during the late 1940s, the Black Russian is a basic blend of two parts vodka to one part Kahlúa. Add heavy cream or milk and it becomes a White Russian (though my version on p. 88 is lighter and more refreshing). The trouble with the Black Russian is that there isn't a whole lot happening. The vodka doesn't bring much more than booziness to the table, which means you're pretty much sipping boosted Kahlúa. The fix, however, is simple. The drink becomes a Brando Russian if you add orange bitters to the mix. That and a splash of orange liqueur are just right to add the balancing bright notes this otherwise simple cocktail needs.

2 ounces vodka

1 ounce Kahlúa

¼ ounce orange liqueur

Dash orange bitters

Ice cubes

In a stirring glass, combine the vodka, Kahlúa, orange liqueur and bitters. Stir with ice cubes, then strain into a rocks glass with 1 large or 2 standard ice cubes.

POUR ME ANOTHER
★ NOW TRY ★

White(-ish) Russian, 88
Frangelic Beauty, 106
Chai Slide, 92
Nutcracker, 132
The Porker, 138
The Dirty Orange, 64

CHAI SLIDE

The Chai Slide is my attempt to make a grown-up Mudslide. The original boozed-up milkshake dates back to Grand Cayman Island in the 1970s, with a mix of vodka, coffee liqueur, Baileys Irish Cream and heavy cream. Oof! My version ditches the heavy, sugary liqueurs in favor of lighter, yet creamy whole milk. Richness comes from chai tea (which also adds complementary spice) and cocoa powder. The result is creamy, sweet and rich without being heavy or cloying.

1 bag chai tea

¼ cup boiling water

3 ounces vodka

1 ounce whole milk

½ ounce agave or simple syrup

⅛ teaspoon unsweetened cocoa powder, plus extra to garnish

Ice cubes

In a cup, combine the tea bag and water. Steep for 2 minutes. Squeeze the tea bag into the cup, then discard. In a cocktail shaker, combine the vodka, tea, milk, syrup and cocoa powder. Shake with ice cubes. Strain into a rocks glass. Lightly dust with cocoa powder.

POUR ME ANOTHER

★ NOW TRY ★

Lime in de Coconut, 83
Coconut-Lime Daiquiri, 199
The Fitzroy, 239
Jalapeño Yuzu Rumtini, 200
Brando Russian, 91
Dolce Vita, 133
Nutcracker, 132
South of the Border, 248
The Porker, 138

SMALL VICTORIES

Credit for the original Small Victories cocktail goes to Alex Day, one of the authors of the brilliant *Cocktail Codex* (a must-have cocktail book) and co-owner of the amazing Death & Co bars in New York and Denver. My adaptation admittedly is a few steps to the side of Day's recipe, which features gin, vodka, root beer–infused Cocchi Americano and marmalade. I was intrigued by the combination of orange, vodka and Cocchi Americano, so that's what I focused on. The result is light, fruity and refreshing.

2½ ounces vodka

2 ounces orange juice

½ ounce Cocchi Americano

¼ ounce agave or simple syrup

Dash orange bitters

Ice cubes

1 orange wedge

In a cocktail shaker, combine the vodka, orange juice, Cocchi Americano, syrup and bitters. Shake with ice cubes, then strain into a rocks glass with 1 large or 2 standard ice cubes. Squeeze the orange wedge over the drink, then add it to the cocktail.

POUR ME ANOTHER
★ NOW TRY ★

Singapore Sling, 41
Flirtini, 94
Dark and Stormy, 187
Tropical Itch, 201
Fog Cutter, 188
Mai Tai, 189
Latin Love, 191

FLIRTINI

Welcome back to the late 20th century! The Flirtini is almost as '90s as the Cosmopolitan. Variations abound, but most combine pineapple juice, orange liqueur and vodka, then top it all with sparkling wine. Dale DeGroff adds fresh pineapple to the mix, muddling it with the orange liqueur. I follow his lead, but leave out the juice, which waters down the finished cocktail. The cherry finish, however, is essential.

¼ cup pineapple chunks

½ ounce orange liqueur

2 ounces vodka

Ice, cubes and crushed

1 maraschino cherry

1 ounce sparkling wine

In a stirring glass, combine the pineapple and orange liqueur. Muddle well. Add the vodka, then stir with ice cubes. Double strain into a coupe filled halfway with crushed ice, then add the cherry. Top with the sparkling wine.

POUR ME ANOTHER

★ NOW TRY ★

Singapore Sling, 41

Small Victories, 93

Dark and Stormy, 187

Tropical Itch, 201

Fog Cutter, 188

Mai Tai, 189

Latin Love, 191

SNEAKY SLEEPER

FRUITY

CREAMY

SWEET

Tea is such an underrated cocktail mixer. And so many of them work—chai, black, green, rooibos. They add wonderful flavor that permeates the cocktail without overwhelming the other ingredients. In this case, I went with gentle and floral chamomile, which pairs wonderfully with the tropical flavor of pineapple juice and sweetness of orange liqueur. The result is frothy, creamy and utterly comforting.

1 bag chamomile tea

¼ cup boiling water

2 ounces vodka

1 ounce pineapple juice

½ ounce orange liqueur

¼ ounce agave or simple syrup

6 to 10 granules kosher salt

Ice cubes

In a cup, combine the tea bag and water. Steep for 2 minutes. Squeeze the tea bag into the cup, then discard. In a cocktail shaker, combine the tea, vodka, pineapple juice, orange liqueur, syrup and salt. Shake with ice cubes, then strain into a rocks glass with 1 large or 2 standard ice cubes.

POUR ME ANOTHER
★ NOW TRY ★

A Day at the Beach, 204
Parisian Blonde, 195
Buttered Rum, 196
Italian Margarita, 242
Air Mail, 197
Amber on the Rocks, 87
White(-ish) Russian, 88
Guadalajara, 243
Painkiller, 194

SEX ON THE BEACH

The Sex on the Beach is one of those mystery cocktails whose origins aren't entirely clear, though it likely dates to the 1960s or 1970s. At first glance, the drink appears to be the summer love child of a Fuzzy Navel (which spikes orange juice with peach schnapps) and a Cape Cod (cranberry juice spiked with vodka). Blend the two and you get your basic Sex on the Beach. My version ditches the peach schnapps because, well, I'm not 18. The cleaner, fruitier flavor of peach juice (also try the mango version, it's killer) is far better.

3 ounces vodka

2 ounces sweetened cranberry
 juice

1 ounce orange juice

1 ounce peach or mango juice

¼ ounce agave or simple syrup

6 to 10 granules kosher salt

Ice cubes

In a cocktail shaker, combine the vodka, cranberry juice, orange juice, peach or mango juice, syrup and salt. Shake with ice cubes, then strain into a coupe.

POUR ME ANOTHER
★ NOW TRY ★

The Sweet Patootie, 50
Roman Punch, 205
Piña Colada, 192
Bennett, 44
Mary Pickford Cocktail, 207
Knickerbocker, 206
Fedora, 208

A SLICE OF PIE

When I was at university, the cool cocktail of the geek set was the Apple Pie Cocktail. Everyone swore that this vodka concoction—an alchemy that varied depending on who was mixing and how much they'd pre-gamed before doing so—tasted exactly like apple pie. While I certainly appreciated the inebriating qualities of those masterpieces, rarely did I feel as though I was slurping a slice. For most of us, drinks such as this fade into a forgotten mist of bad choices. But in a nostalgic fit, I decided to try to one-up my college self and see if this time I really could create a cocktail that tastes like it sounds. I'll let you be the judge. If you really want to channel those collegiate vibes, serve in a red Solo cup.

1½ ounces vodka
1 tablespoon frozen apple juice
    concentrate
½ ounce apple brandy

¼ ounce crème de cacao
¼ ounce Licor 43
Dash orange bitters
Ice cubes

In a stirring glass, combine the vodka, apple juice concentrate, brandy, crème de cacao, Licor 43 and bitters. Stir with ice cubes, then strain into a rocks glass with 1 large or 2 standard ice cubes.

POUR ME ANOTHER

★ NOW TRY ★

Piña Colada, 192
Bennett, 44
Knickerbocker, 206
Fedora, 208
Mary Pickford Cocktail, 207
Sex on the Beach, 96
Roman Punch, 205

IMPROVED SCREWDRIVER

FRUITY
SWEET
STRONG

Most Screwdrivers are simple combinations of orange juice and vodka, which to me isn't much more than a flavorless, flat Mimosa. But if you dig into the history of the drink, options abound for taking things in more interesting directions. The Screwdriver is a sibling of the Orange Blossom, which is gin, orange juice and a bit of sugar. Sub vodka for the gin and you've got an early-era Screwdriver. But David Embury wrote about two other relatives that offer a bit more depth. There is the Volga, which reverses the equation to up the vodka and decrease the juice, then adds grenadine, lime juice and orange bitters to the mix. The Volga Boatman streamlines to call for only vodka, orange juice and cherry liqueur. My version borrows from all three. I opt for the sugar of the Orange Blossom, which helps balance a longer pour of vodka. With all that sweetness, grenadine isn't needed, but I kept the lime juice from the Volga. And because it adds a fruity complexity otherwise lacking, I added the cherry liqueur from the Volga Boatman.

2½ ounces vodka

1 ounce orange juice

¼ ounce maraschino liqueur

¼ ounce agave or simple syrup

⅛ ounce (¾ teaspoon) lime juice

6 to 10 granules kosher salt

Ice cubes

In a cocktail shaker, combine the vodka, orange juice, maraschino liqueur, syrup, lime juice and salt. Shake with ice cubes, then strain into a cocktail glass.

BLUE MONDAY COCKTAIL

FRUITY

SWEET

REFRESHING

Taking a few liberties with this one. Harry Craddock wrote about this mostly unimpressive little number back in the 1930s. At the time, it was little more than vodka, orange liqueur and—wait for it!—blue food coloring. Yum! Most versions today achieve the desired hue via a splash of blue Curaçao. To me, that's a little too much orange flavor for a drink without a lot else going on. So I decided to take a fruity turn and infuse the vodka with blueberries, a nice balance to the orange liqueur. The result is fresh, bright and fruity rather than a one-note orange bomb. The Peychaud's bitters add both complexity and floral notes that play to all the other flavors.

3 tablespoons blueberries

2 ounces vodka

1 ounce orange liqueur

6 to 10 granules kosher salt

Dash Peychaud's bitters

Ice cubes

In a blender, combine the blueberries, vodka, orange liqueur and salt. Pulse until the blueberries are just finely chopped, but not pureed. Let rest for 1 minute. Double strain into a stirring glass, using a spoon to press on the solids to extract as much liquid as possible. Add the bitters, then stir with ice cubes. Strain into a cocktail glass.

POUR ME ANOTHER

★ NOW TRY ★

Ginger Screw, 101
Improved Screwdriver, 98
Piña Colada, 192
Bennett, 44
Knickerbocker, 206
Fedora, 208
Sex on the Beach, 96
Mary Pickford Cocktail, 207
A Slice of Pie, 97
Roman Punch, 205

MR. 404

The oddly named Mr. 404 cocktail delivers bold flavor and color, both of which can be attributed largely to the Aperol. I'm a sucker for any cocktail that balances bitter and refreshing flavors. It's a marriage that in many ways makes this cocktail a distant relative of the Aperol Spritz. The Mr. 404, however, packs a bit more punch, a characteristic masked by the floral notes of the elderflower liqueur.

1½ ounces vodka

½ ounce elderflower liqueur

½ ounce Aperol

¼ ounce lemon juice

⅛ ounce (¾ teaspoon) agave or simple syrup

Ice cubes

Orange zest twist

In a cocktail shaker, combine the vodka, elderflower liqueur, Aperol, lemon juice and syrup. Shake with ice cubes, then strain into a cocktail glass. Garnish with the orange twist.

POUR ME ANOTHER

★ NOW TRY ★

Ginger Screw, 101
Piña Colada, 192
Bennett, 44
Knickerbocker, 206
Fedora, 208
Sex on the Beach, 96
Mary Pickford Cocktail, 207
A Slice of Pie, 97
Roman Punch, 205

GINGER SCREW

Orange juice plus alcohol. It's a much-loved equation. Sparkling wine gives you a Mimosa. Gin gives you an Orange Blossom. And, of course, vodka gives you a Screwdriver. My Improved Screwdriver (p. 98) borrows from related cocktails to gussy up the basic equation with maraschino liqueur and lime juice. But the Screwdriver is a drink that's been reinvented a million ways. For this simple iteration, I wanted bright, punchy notes, so I added peppery ginger. I also tinkered with the ratio to give the liquor more presence than the juice. Because I'm THAT sort of guy.

2 ounces vodka

1 ounce orange juice

½ ounce ginger liqueur

6 to 10 granules kosher salt

Ice cubes

In a cocktail shaker, combine the vodka, orange juice, ginger liqueur and salt. Shake with ice cubes, then strain into a cocktail glass.

POUR ME ANOTHER
★ NOW TRY ★

Satan's Whiskers, 45
Slow Screw Missionary Style, 47
Roman Punch, 205
Harvey Wallbanger, 103
Piña Colada, 192
Bennett, 44
Knickerbocker, 206
Fedora, 208
Sex on the Beach, 96
Mary Pickford Cocktail, 207
A Slice of Pie, 97

VODKA FIX

This is my vodka take on the Gin Fix, a relative of the Gin Daisy. Six degrees of separation is such a fun game to play… The basic Daisy is gin, lemon or lime juice and grenadine. The basic Fix swaps pineapple syrup for the grenadine. When David Embury made his Gin Fix, he suggested an optional spoonful of herbal Green Chartreuse added at the very end. I liked all that, but wanted to get the gin out of the equation so the Green Chartreuse and pineapple could take center stage (thanks to a strong supporting role by vodka). The result is astoundingly smooth.

3 ounces vodka
1 ounce pineapple juice
¼ ounce Green Chartreuse
¼ ounce lime juice

¼ ounce orgeat syrup
6 to 10 granules kosher salt
Ice cubes

In a cocktail shaker, combine the vodka, pineapple juice, Green Chartreuse, lime juice, orgeat syrup and salt. Shake with ice cubes, then strain into a coupe.

POUR ME ANOTHER
★ NOW TRY ★

Corpse Reviver, 48
The Monkey Gland, 51
Gin Daisy, 57
Paloma, 255
Navy Grog, 222
Maragato Cocktail, 209

HARVEY WALLBANGER

The original Harvey Wallbanger, which was created in the 1950s, is basically a Screwdriver (vodka and orange juice) adulterated with Galliano, an Italian liqueur with sweet, herbal and vanilla notes. It typically is served in a highball, but I wanted to go low. This allows me to reduce the orange juice, which can add too much sweetness and dilute the Galliano. So rather than use juice, I muddle an orange slice with agave. Stir with vodka and Galliano and suddenly Harvey is feeling sophisticated.

½-inch-thick orange round

¼ ounce agave or simple syrup

2 ounces vodka

1 ounce Galliano

Ice cubes

In a stirring glass, muddle the orange round and agave. Add the vodka and Galliano, then stir with ice cubes. Strain into a rocks glass with 1 large or 2 standard ice cubes.

POUR ME ANOTHER

★ NOW TRY ★

Ginger Screw, 101
Improved Screwdriver, 98

FRENCH MARTINI

Though there are several iterations of the French Martini, credit for this subclass of the basic Martini goes to New York City restaurateur Keith McNally. His Balthazar restaurant popularized it—and its many flavored cousins to follow. Some versions are little more than vodka and raspberry liqueur. Many add pineapple juice. Some swap gin for the vodka. Almost as important as what goes into it are the proportions. The additions should simply suggest flavors, not bash you over the head with them.

2 ounces vodka

¼ ounce pineapple juice

¼ ounce raspberry liqueur

6 to 10 granules kosher salt

Ice cubes

In a cocktail shaker, combine the vodka, pineapple juice, raspberry liqueur and salt. Shake with ice cubes, then strain into a cocktail glass.

POUR ME ANOTHER

★ NOW TRY ★

The Aviation, 37
Gin and Tonic, 27
One Cool Cucumber, 227

CREAMSICLE

SWEET
CREAMY
FRUITY
REFRESHING

No way around it—the Creamsicle is the sort of trashy cocktail you drink to feel better and then worse about yourself. All without regrets. There isn't a whole lot of sophistication happening here— just creamy, sweet and juicy goodness. And yes, it tastes precisely as it sounds. Consider the ginger liqueur optional. I like the bright pepperiness it adds; it's a great contrast to all the sweet-creamy action happening here.

2 ounces vodka

½ ounce orange liqueur

½ ounce ginger liqueur

1 tablespoon frozen orange juice concentrate

6 to 10 granules kosher salt

Ice cubes

¼ cup vanilla ice cream

In a stirring glass, combine the vodka, orange liqueur, ginger liqueur, orange juice concentrate and salt. Add 2 standard ice cubes, then stir until the concentrate is fully dissolved. Scoop the ice cream into a coupe. Strain the cocktail over the ice cream, then carefully use your fingers to spin the glass by its stem to create trails of melting ice cream in the drink.

POUR ME ANOTHER

★ NOW TRY ★

The Fitzroy, 239
Jungle Bird, 225
Kretchma, 86
Coffee Cargo Cocktail, 122
Spiced Orange Daiquiri, 193

FRANGELIC BEAUTY

Consider the Frangelic Beauty to be a creamier, less brooding Espresso Martini. Frangelico is a sweet Italian liqueur made from hazelnuts. It gives vodka creamy depth and richness, minus the bitter, caffeinated punch of espresso. The result is warming without being heavy. For a brighter take on this, swap orange bitters for the Angostura.

2 ounces vodka

1 ounce Frangelico

¼ ounce dry vermouth

⅛ ounce (¾ teaspoon) agave or
   simple syrup

Dash Angostura bitters

6 to 10 granules kosher salt

Ice cubes

In a cocktail shaker, combine the vodka, Frangelico, vermouth, syrup, bitters and salt. Shake with ice cubes, then strain into a Nick and Nora glass.

POUR ME ANOTHER
★ NOW TRY ★

Espresso Martini, 123
Coffee Cargo Cocktail, 122
Aztec's Mark, 154
White(-ish) Russian, 88
Chai Slide, 92
Nutcracker, 132
The Porker, 138
The Dirty Orange, 64

BOOZY SMOOTHIE

This is what happens when your morning smoothie wakes up ready to party. True to its name, this one drinks pretty smoothly, so watch out. Also, feel free to play with the fruit combinations. Frozen mango, peaches or strawberries can be substituted for the banana and pineapple.

3 ounces vodka

2 ounces coconut water

2-inch chunk frozen banana

¼ cup frozen pineapple chunks

¼ ounce agave or simple syrup

6 to 10 granules kosher salt

In a blender, combine the vodka, coconut water, banana, pineapple, syrup and salt. Blend until smooth, then pour into a coupe or rocks glass.

POUR ME ANOTHER
* NOW TRY *

The Derby, 140
Crimean Cup à La Marmora, 221
Cossack, 82
Gloom Chaser, 220
All Jammed Up, 108
Lemon Drop, 117
The Big Apple, 139

ALL JAMMED UP

I'm a big fan of using jam to flavor cocktails. It can be a power house ingredient, adding sweetness, viscosity and flavor. The honest way to craft this cocktail is to use a jam jar that has just the scrapings left in it. That's usually the perfect amount to flavor the drink and it lets you use the jar as both the shaker and the serving glass. But if you don't have that handy, just a spoonful of jam and a traditional cocktail shaker will get the job done. While I prefer raspberry jam for this recipe, use any flavor you like.

2½ ounces vodka
¼ ounce orange liqueur
¼ ounce Ancho Reyes

1 teaspoon raspberry jam
Ice cubes

In a cocktail shaker, combine the vodka, orange liqueur, Ancho Reyes and jam. Shake with ice cubes, then double strain into a cocktail glass with 1 large or 2 standard ice cubes.

POUR ME ANOTHER
★ NOW TRY ★

The Derby, 140
Crimean Cup à La Marmora, 221
Cossack, 82
Boozy Smoothie, 107
Gloom Chaser, 220
Lemon Drop, 117
The Big Apple, 139

CHERRY-LIME VODKA RICKEY

SWEET
SOUR
REFRESHING

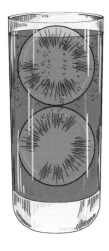

A Rickey is the perfect summer drink—bright, refreshing, sweet and sour. The original uses gin, lime, sugar and club soda. But that Gimlet-like formula is the perfect vehicle for a bit of vodka. My goal with this version was to capture the (nonalcoholic) cherry-lime rickeys served by the ice cream shop near my childhood home. The addition of a little maraschino cherry syrup (from a jar of maraschino cherries) nails it perfectly. Make sure you are using real maraschino cherry syrup here, not the liquid from those Day-Glo cherries sold at the grocery store. Luxardo and Fabbri Amarena are excellent choices.

3 ounces vodka

1 ounce lime juice

¼ ounce agave or simple syrup

¼ ounce maraschino cherry
 syrup

Ice cubes

2 ounces seltzer water

In a highball or generous rocks glass, combine the vodka, lime juice, agave or simple syrup and cherry syrup. Stir, then add 2 large or 4 standard ice cubes. Top with the seltzer water.

POUR ME ANOTHER
★ NOW TRY ★

Vodka Gimlet, 118
Bee's Knees, 52
Vodka Caipirinha, 115

VODKA SPECIAL

David Embury's Vodka Special calls for vodka, crème de cacao and lemon juice. But he notes a variation that replaces the crème de cacao with maraschino liqueur and the lemon juice with lime. And that cocktail walks nearly lockstep with a Vodka Gimlet, the difference being the maraschino liqueur. That difference adds a gentle fruity quality that tones down the bracing acidity of the lime.

2 ounces vodka
½ ounce maraschino liqueur
¼ ounce lime juice

¼ ounce agave or simple syrup
6 to 10 granules kosher salt
Ice cubes

In a cocktail shaker, combine the vodka, maraschino liqueur, lime juice, syrup and salt. Shake with ice cubes, then strain into a cocktail glass.

POUR ME ANOTHER
★ NOW TRY ★

Inca, 55
El Presidente Cocktail, 224
Vodka Gimlet, 118
Pendennis Club, 69
classic Daiquiri, 183
Loud Speaker, 67

COSMOPOLITAN

SWEET

SOUR

REFRESHING

STRONG

Seems just about everyone wants to take credit for creating the Cosmopolitan. Some stories date to the 1930s, others wind their way through Provincetown's roaring gay scene. Rather than expend too much energy teasing out the truth, let's focus instead on making a better Cosmo. The modern classic, which Joe and Daniel Schofield attribute to Toby Cecchini at New York's The Odeon in 1988, is citrus-flavored vodka, orange liqueur, lime juice, sugar and cranberry juice. Many lesser bars ditch the sugar and tannic cranberry juice in favor of sweetened cranberry juice cocktail. But I find that can turn the drink into a sugary mess. So I decided to get flavor from the source—fresh cranberries. Using the blender, it's easy to speed-infuse vodka with fresh cranberries. That also turns out to be a better way to make citrus vodka, so I add a generous strip of lemon zest to the blender, too. Once infused, it's a simple matter of shaking the vodka with agave syrup and lime juice.

3 ounces vodka

¼ cup fresh or frozen (thawed) cranberries

2-inch strip lemon zest

½ ounce orange liqueur

½ ounce agave or simple syrup

¼ ounce lime juice

Ice cubes

POUR ME ANOTHER

★ NOW TRY ★

Bay Breeze, 80
Sex on the Beach, 96
Bee's Knees, 52
Vodka Caipirinha, 115
Cherry-Lime Vodka Rickey, 109
Vodka Gimlet, 118

In a blender, combine the vodka, cranberries and lemon zest. Pulse just until the cranberries and zest are well chopped, but not pureed. Let steep for 1 minute. Double strain into a cocktail shaker, using a spoon to press on the solids to extract as much liquid as possible. Add the orange liqueur, syrup and lime juice. Shake with ice cubes, then strain into a cocktail glass.

POOH BEAR

Honey and herbs play so well together, I couldn't resist combining the flavors in a cocktail. The honey is easy. As for the herbal notes, I went with Galliano, an Italian liqueur created around the turn of the 20th century. Its floral sweetness and gentle herbal and vanilla notes make it the perfect companion for honey. Coconut water keeps things light and tropical and orange bitters add brightness without changing the acidity or sweetness of the cocktail.

1 ounce coconut water
½ ounce honey
2 ounces vodka

½ ounce Galliano
Dash orange bitters
Ice cubes

In a stirring glass, combine the coconut water and honey. Stir until the honey is dissolved. Add the vodka, Galliano and bitters. Stir with ice cubes. Strain into a rocks glass with 1 standard ice cube.

POUR ME ANOTHER
★ NOW TRY ★

Tequila Poncha, 252

RIO JENGIBRE

This cocktail is loosely inspired by the tequila drink Rio Bravo, a blend of tequila, lime juice and ginger beer, sometimes with strawberries muddled in. I love the peppery-tangy flavor profile of lime and ginger together, but I didn't want that to compete with tequila. Enter vodka! For cleaner, crisper ginger flavor, I opted for fresh ginger, which is muddled with an orange zest strip. The result is bright and a little (pleasantly) biting.

Orange zest strip	¼ ounce lime juice
2 coins fresh ginger	3 ounces vodka
½ ounce agave or simple syrup	Ice, cubes and crushed

In a cocktail shaker, combine the zest strip, ginger, syrup and lime juice. Muddle. Add the vodka. Shake with ice cubes, then double strain into a coupe filled halfway with crushed ice.

POUR ME ANOTHER
★ NOW TRY ★

Guadalajara, 243
Parisian Blonde, 195
Buttered Rum, 196
Italian Margarita, 242

LONG ISLAND ICED TEA

I'm sorry, but I'm going to say it. The Long Island Iced Tea is the trash can of cocktails. Throw everything into a glass and swill it down. That said, a GOOD Long Island Iced Tea is possible. But it requires balance. Original recipes date to at least the 1970s, but some say it may even go back to the 1920s, when another five-liquor cocktail was making the rounds. Either way, there simply is so much going on, you need to be mindful that no one ingredient outshines another. Typically, this is a long pour served in a highball. But that requires either an unhealthy amount of booze, an unpleasant amount of ice or a stupid amount of cola. My version allows the different liquors to actually have a presence in the drink. The result is sweet and strong and pleasantly boozy.

1 ounce vodka

½ ounce blanco tequila

½ ounce gin

½ ounce white rum

¼ ounce orange liqueur

¼ ounce agave or simple syrup

¼ ounce lemon juice

Ice cubes

2 ounces cola soda

In a cocktail shaker, combine the vodka, tequila, gin, rum, orange liqueur, syrup and lemon juice. Shake with ice cubes, then strain into a rocks glass with 1 large or 2 standard ice cubes. Top with the cola.

POUR ME ANOTHER

★ NOW TRY ★

Isla Grande Iced Tea, 261
Ginger Screw, 101
Improved Screwdriver, 98
Blue Monday Cocktail, 99
Bennett, 44
Knickerbocker, 206
Fedora, 208
Sex on the Beach, 96
Mary Pickford Cocktail, 207
A Slice of Pie, 97
Roman Punch, 205

VODKA CAIPIRINHA

SOUR
REFRESHING
SWEET
HERBAL

Substitute vodka for the cachaça in your basic Caipirinha and you end up with a cocktail that is less sweet, a change that allows the sour and refreshing notes of the lime to shine. As with the classic Caipirinha, I make this in a jam or canning jar. That's because it's one of the few drinks served with the ice it is shaken with. Using a jar with a tight lid makes it a simple shake-unscrew-drink affair, no extra glass needed.

1 lime, cut into quarters

1 sprig fresh mint

½ ounce agave or simple syrup

2½ ounces vodka

½ ounce ginger liqueur

Ice cubes

In a jam jar, combine the lime, mint and syrup. Muddle. Add the vodka, ginger liqueur and 6 standard ice cubes. Tightly seal the jar, then shake well. Uncover and serve directly from the jar.

POUR ME ANOTHER

★ NOW TRY ★

Mandarin Tequila Caipirinha, 260
Mojito, 186
Bee's Knees, 52
Navy Grog, 222

VODKA SALTY DOG

The Vodka Salty Dog is a rare exception to my no-salted-rims rule. The cocktail started life as the Greyhound during the 1930s, when Harry Craddock mixed grapefruit and vodka or gin. A few decades later, somebody swapped in vodka for the gin, added salt to the rim of the glass and the Salty Dog was born. Typically, salting the rim of a cocktail glass is a horrible idea; it blows out your ability to taste what's inside the glass. This is particularly true of margaritas, where you want to appreciate the smoky nuances of the tequila against the bright notes of lime. The Vodka Salty Dog, however, is a different animal. With the main (and often only) liquor being vodka, there isn't a lot of nuance happening. Add bracingly tart grapefruit juice and that's pretty much all you're going to taste. So in this case, salt actually both brightens and balances the juice. For a little interest and rounding sweetness, I also add hints of orange liqueur and Aperol. Both play perfect background notes in this modern classic.

Kosher salt

3 ounces grapefruit juice

2 ounces vodka

½ ounce orange liqueur

¼ ounce Aperol

Ice cubes

POUR ME ANOTHER

★ NOW TRY ★

Salty Dog, 54
Lemon Drop, 117

Lightly moisten the rim of a rocks glass with water or citrus juice. Overturn the glass into a plate of kosher salt, moving it around to coat. Turn right-side up and add 1 large or 2 standard ice cubes. In a cocktail shaker, combine the grapefruit juice, vodka, orange liqueur and Aperol. Shake with ice cubes, then strain into the glass.

LEMON DROP

Most people credit the creation of the Lemon Drop to Norman Jay Hobday, a San Francisco bar owner from the 1970s. And likely that's the case, at least in terms of the modern Lemon Drop. But the fine folks at Liquor.com note that it bears striking similarities to the Crusta, a drink that goes back more than 100 years prior. The basic Crusta, which can be made with any core liquor, lines the inside of a glass with the peel of an entire lemon (or sometimes orange) cut in a spiral. Bitters and maraschino liqueur round it out. Hobday's vodka version ditched bitters, swapped orange liqueur for the maraschino, and added as much as a full ounce of sugar. Hence, most Lemon Drops today are sugar bombs. I wanted a lighter, brighter, less sugary cocktail. I kept the bitters and maraschino from the Crusta, but cut the sugar way back. Instead, I get a little sweetness and a pop of additional lemon flavor from limoncello. Coconut water adds a pleasant tropical note that keeps the cocktail from being too sweet.

2-inch lemon zest strip

2 ounces vodka

1 ounce coconut water

¾ ounce lemon juice

½ ounce limoncello

¼ ounce maraschino liqueur

¼ ounce agave or simple syrup

Dash Angostura bitters

Ice cubes

Rub the lemon zest strip around the rim of a coupe, then add it to the glass. In a cocktail shaker, combine the vodka, coconut water, lemon juice, limoncello, maraschino liqueur, syrup and bitters. Shake with ice cubes, then strain into the glass.

POUR ME ANOTHER

✱ NOW TRY ✱

Vodka Special, 110
El Presidente Cocktail, 224
One Cool Cucumber, 227
Inca, 55
Gin Sling, 66
Ko Adang, 213

VODKA GIMLET

The basic Gimlet historically was an equal marriage of gin and lime juice, sometimes with sweetener. More recently, the lime has been toned down to let the gin shine. In 1930, Harry Craddock offered a vodka version of the drink that sported slightly more vodka than lime juice, plus powdered sugar. I tried that. Nope. Powdered sugar, it turns out, doesn't treat cocktails well—it just gets muddy and messy. But swapping in agave or simple syrup and toning down the lime a bit does deliver a splendid cocktail.

2½ ounces vodka

½ ounce lime juice

½ ounce agave or simple syrup

6 to 10 granules kosher salt

Ice cubes

1 lime wedge

In a cocktail shaker, combine the vodka, lime juice, syrup and salt. Shake with ice cubes, then strain into a cocktail glass garnished with a lime wedge.

POUR ME ANOTHER

★ NOW TRY ★

Vodka Special, 110
El Presidente Cocktail, 224
One Cool Cucumber, 227
Inca, 55

HEAVY WEATHER

SOUR
SWEET
STRONG
CREAMY

This cocktail is loosely based on one of the same name served at the lovely bar Portland Hunt + Alpine Club in Portland, Maine. It's a tiki-adjacent drink that they serve with a tiny umbrella, a reference to the name of the cocktail. The use of allspice in a cocktail is a game changer. Subtle richness, spice and depth, all from barely a pinch. The result is wonderfully, unexpectedly creamy. When measuring a "bare pinch," aim for the amount you would get between just the tips of two fingers. A little bit goes a long way.

3 ounces vodka

2 ounces grapefruit juice

¼ ounce agave or simple syrup

Bare pinch ground allspice

Ice cubes

In a cocktail shaker, combine the vodka, grapefruit juice, syrup and allspice. Shake with ice cubes, then strain into a rocks glass with 1 large or 2 standard ice cubes.

POUR ME ANOTHER

★ NOW TRY ★

Gin Sling, 66
Ko Adang, 213

KATINKA

SOUR
SWEET
STRONG

Though several drinks go by the name Katinka, the most common and delicious blends vodka, apricot liqueur and lime juice. It's a simple equation that's probably 100 or so years old, but these days doesn't get a lot of attention. I love the simplicity of it, but found it needed some help to taste balanced. A little extra sugar and a dash of bitters was just about right.

2 ounces vodka

½ ounce apricot liqueur

¼ ounce lime juice

¼ ounce agave or simple syrup

Dash Angostura bitters

6 to 10 granules kosher salt

Ice cubes

In a cocktail shaker, combine the vodka, apricot liqueur, lime juice, syrup, bitters and salt. Shake with ice cubes, then strain into a Nick and Nora glass.

POUR ME ANOTHER

★ NOW TRY ★

Long Island Iced Tea, 114
Ginger Screw, 101
Improved Screwdriver, 98
Blue Monday Cocktail, 99
Piña Colada, 192
Bennett, 44
Knickerbocker, 206
Fedora, 208
Sex on the Beach, 96
Mary Pickford Cocktail, 207
A Slice of Pie, 97
Roman Punch, 205

WELL-SPOKEN RUSSIAN

A classic The Last Word, which dates to around Prohibition, calls for equal parts gin, Green Chartreuse, maraschino liqueur and lime juice. Over time, those proportions generally tilted to favor the gin, which otherwise was too easily overwhelmed by the other liquors. In this vodka version of The Last Word, we let the Green Chartreuse and maraschino liqueur fly their freak flags high; the neutral vodka allows them to shine without worry of competing against any other flavors. The result is wonderfully herbal and gently sweet.

1 ounce vodka

1 ounce Green Chartreuse

½ ounce maraschino liqueur

Ice, cubes and crushed

In a cocktail shaker, combine the vodka, Green Chartreuse and maraschino liqueur. Shake with ice cubes, then strain into a coupe filled halfway with crushed ice.

POUR ME ANOTHER
★ NOW TRY ★

The Last Word, 72
The Horse Thief, 59
Hanky Panky, 60
La Ultima Palabra, 256

COFFEE CARGO COCKTAIL

STRONG
CREAMY

In 1930, Harry Craddock wrote about a drink called the White Cargo Cocktail, a simple 50-50 shaken blend of vanilla ice cream and gin. Frankly, the idea of gin and ice cream really didn't resonate with me. But it did inspire this espresso-based cocktail. Think of it as an Espresso Martini that uses vanilla ice cream in place of ice.

¼ cup vanilla ice cream

2 ounces vodka

1 ounce Kahlúa

2 ounces espresso, cooled

In a stirring glass, combine the ice cream, vodka, Kahlúa and espresso. Stir for 1 minute, or until the ice cream has melted. Pour into a coupe.

POUR ME ANOTHER
★ NOW TRY ★

Espresso Martini, 123
The Mule's Hind Leg, 65
Creamsicle, 105

ESPRESSO MARTINI

STRONG

CREAMY

SWEET

BITTER

The Espresso Martini is a relative newcomer to the cocktail world. It was created by Dick Bradsell at Soho Brasserie in London during the early 1980s. Supposedly, it was crafted for a model who asked for a drink that would equally perk her up and f*** her up. Got to love a good origin story. As ever, a great Espresso Martini is all about balance. Ample pours of vodka, coffee liqueur and espresso are key; the pinch of salt highlights the delicious natural bitterness of the espresso. Don't be tempted to add sugar—it will mask the flavors of the other ingredients. The Kahlúa has all the sweetness you need.

2½ ounces vodka

1½ ounces Kahlúa

2 ounces brewed espresso, cooled

6 to 10 granules kosher salt

Ice cubes

In a cocktail shaker, combine the vodka, Kahlúa, espresso and salt. Shake with ice cubes. Strain into a coupe or cocktail glass.

POUR ME ANOTHER

★ NOW TRY ★

Coffee Cargo Cocktail, 122
Frangelic Beauty, 106
Aztec's Mark, 154
The Mule's Hind Leg, 65

VODKA OLD FASHIONED

STRONG

FRUITY

SWEET

Minimalism is key when turning vodka into an Old Fashioned. The neutral strength of the vodka means too much of any other ingredient easily pushes the cocktail off balance. So a light hand with the sugar is essential. I like the combination of both Angostura and orange bitters, but one or the other is fine. Also, since it is allowed to shine loud and clear, the vodka really ought to be top-notch for this drink.

1 orange zest strip

Ice cubes

3 ounces premium vodka

⅛ ounce (¾ teaspoon) agave or
   simple syrup

Dash Angostura bitters

Dash orange bitters

6 to 10 granules kosher salt

Rub the orange zest strip around the rim of a cocktail glass, then add it to the glass with 1 large or 2 standard ice cubes. In a stirring glass, combine the vodka, syrup, both bitters and salt. Stir with ice cubes, then strain into the glass.

POUR ME ANOTHER

★ NOW TRY ★

Whiskey Old Fashioned, 131
Rum Old Fashioned, 229
Orange Martini, 68

YELLOW PARROT

This intense cocktail first shows up in print in 1922. Robert Vermeire calls for equal parts absinthe, Yellow Chartreuse and apricot brandy. The result is beautiful and deliciously herbal and sweet, but can be a little too bold. A lot of folks suggest stirring it for a full minute to dilute it. I prefer a normal stir and adding just a bit of vodka, which creates a neutral canvas on which all the other flavors can shine.

¾ ounce vodka

¾ ounce absinthe

¾ ounce Yellow Chartreuse

¾ ounce apricot brandy

Ice cubes

In a stirring glass, combine the vodka, absinthe, Yellow Chartreuse and brandy. Stir with ice cubes, then strain into a cocktail glass.

POUR ME ANOTHER

★ NOW TRY ★

Hanky Panky, 60
The Last Word, 72
Well-Spoken Russian, 121
1920 Pick-Me-Up, 73
Martinez, 74
La Ultima Palabra, 256
Zombie, 231

MINT FIZZ

STRONG

HERBAL
REFRESHING

SOUR

Fizz cocktails have been kicking around for more than 150 years. The best known is the Gin Fizz, an offshoot of Sour cocktails. It combines the obvious liquor with citrus juice, sugar and some variant of carbonated water or soda. This variation on the Fizz calls for vodka, which allows the freshness of the mint and the brightness of the lemon juice to shine. Orgeat adds viscosity and a gentle almond creaminess, but you could use agave or simple syrup, too. Resist the urge to double strain the drink. The flecks of mint give the cocktail a beautiful speckled look.

2 sprigs fresh mint

½ ounce orgeat syrup

3 ounces vodka

¼ ounce lemon juice

Ice, cubes and crushed

1 ounce club soda

In a cocktail shaker, combine the mint and orgeat syrup. Muddle. Leave the muddler in the shaker. Add the vodka and lemon juice, then swish the muddler to rinse. Remove the muddler. Shake with ice cubes. Strain into a coupe filled halfway with crushed ice. Top with club soda.

POUR ME ANOTHER

★ NOW TRY ★

Gin Fizz, 35
The Last Word, 72
Well-Spoken Russian, 121
1920 Pick-Me-Up, 73
Martinez, 74
Yellow Parrot, 125
La Ultima Palabra, 256
Zombie, 231

BRIGHTON BEACH

STRONG

HERBAL

SWEET

This relative of the classic Manhattan is less brooding than the original, the vodka lightening the load a bit. Meanwhile, the sweet vermouth and Green Chartreuse add sweet herbal notes that bring complexity without being cloying.

2 ounces vodka

1 ounce sweet vermouth

½ ounce Green Chartreuse

Dash Angostura bitters

Ice cubes

1 maraschino cherry

In a rocks glass, combine the vodka, sweet vermouth, Green Chartreuse and bitters. Stir with 1 large or 2 standard ice cubes. Add the cherry.

POUR ME ANOTHER

★ NOW TRY ★

Manhattan, 153

Martinez, 74

The Last Word, 72

Well-Spoken Russian, 121

1920 Pick-Me-Up, 73

La Ultima Palabra, 256

Sazerac, 175

MOSCOW MULE

STRONG
_____
SPICY
_____
SOUR

The Moscow Mule was born around 1941, apparently in an effort to correct some poor purchasing decisions. Though some of the history is disputed, one thing most folks agree on is that the goal was to use up a vodka surplus. One telling of the story is that the Heublein Spirits company had acquired the rights to Smirnoff vodka, but overestimated the American appetite for it at the time. Throw in a bartender who had purchased too much ginger beer, then toss in the bartender's girlfriend, who supposedly owned a company that made copper mugs… And, well, there's your Moscow Mule.

Whatever the origins, the trick to crafting a proper Moscow Mule is keeping the lime juice in check so it doesn't obliterate the clean, brightly peppery notes of the ginger. Classic recipes tended to go way overboard on the lime. For the ginger, I decided to go back to the source—fresh ginger root—instead of ginger beer. Using the blender, I create a speed infusion with the vodka, giving the finished cocktail a bold, clean ginger presence. A finishing squeeze of lime juice is all that's needed to brighten everything.

POUR ME ANOTHER

★ NOW TRY ★

King Cole Cocktail, 178
Flu Cocktail, 179
Kentucky Longshot, 151

3 ounces vodka

1-inch chunk fresh ginger

2-inch strip lime zest

¼ ounce agave or simple syrup

6 to 10 granules kosher salt

Ice cubes

Dash Angostura bitters

1 lime wedge

In a blender, combine the vodka, ginger and lime zest. Pulse just until the ginger and zest are well chopped, but not pureed. Let steep for 1 minute. Double strain into a cocktail shaker, using a spoon to press the solids to extract as much liquid as possible. Add the syrup and salt, then shake with ice cubes. Strain into a coupe. Top with the bitters, then squeeze the lime wedge over the drink and add it to it.

WHISKEY
(BOURBON AND RYE)

Rye and bourbon are born STRONG and WARM, but they don't have to stay that way. Pineapple juice and bitters or absinthe take your whiskey into downright FRUITY and HERBAL territory as a LINSTEAD COCKTAIL. Your basic OLD FASHIONED—which should be nothing more than whiskey, sugar and bitters—also goes all HERBAL and even a little REFRESHING when you add the foliage needed for a MINT JULEP. Want to stay STRONG? Obviously, a bit of sweet vermouth transforms the OLD FASHIONED into a MANHATTAN. But take that MANHATTAN and add some hazelnut Frangelico and now you've got a CREAMY DOLCE VITA. Brown liquor isn't nearly as brooding as you think.

Astute whiskey drinkers will notice the absence of Scotch and Irish whiskey in this chapter. That's because I find that their more pronounced flavor notes are challenging for home mixologists to balance. I stuck with the most reliable mixers—lightly sweet bourbon and gently peppery rye. If you want to dabble on the smoky side, opt for low-peat Scotches, such as Monkey Shoulder. Strong peaty flavors can overwhelm a cocktail. And if smoke is your jam, be sure to check out the mezcal recipes, which deliver similar flavor notes.

When stocking your bar for whiskey cocktails, the middle shelf generally is your best friend. I'm reliably happy with bottles in the $20 to $40 range. And almost anything from Bulleit, Jefferson's or Four Roses is a solid bet. My exception to my rule? When I want a VIEUX CARRÉ or MANHATTAN that takes me to the next level, I splurge on a bottle of Jefferson's Straight Rye Whiskey Finished in Cognac Casks. It's double the price and worth seeking out for those special days.

OLD FASHIONED

STRONG
WARM

SWEET
SPICY
FRUITY

The Old Fashioned is one of those cocktails that truly has been through the wringer. Many of the oldest recipes are nothing more than some indiscriminate whiskey with a sugar cube and bitters, sometimes a splash of water. A few recipes, as in Harry Johnson's 1882 *Bartenders' Manual,* added a dash of absinthe or Curaçao to the mix "if required," as he said. Things went along merrily until Prohibition meant the rotgut Americans were forced to drink no longer could be appreciated in such simple form. Cue the addition of fruit to the Old Fashioned. In time, that became the standard, and sadly so. But in recent years, we've seen a return of the so-called pre-Prohibition-era Old Fashioned. Thankfully! This is my very simple take on that classic. I'm adamant about not adding much ice to my Old Fashioned, but adjust as you see fit.

3 ounces bourbon or rye

⅛ ounce (¾ teaspoon) agave or
   simple syrup

Dash orange or Angostura
   bitters

1 small ice cube

In a rocks glass, stir the bourbon, syrup, bitters and ice cube.

POUR ME ANOTHER

★ NOW TRY ★

Rum Old Fashioned, 229
Vodka Old Fashioned, 124
Manhattan, 153
Poker Cocktail, 226
Mississippi Punch, 232
Mexican Old Fashioned, 249
Bijou, 58
Vieux Carré, 180

NUTCRACKER

This is a case of something so right going so wrong. The good news is that with a little paring back, the best elements of this creamy and strong cocktail are able to shine. Many versions of the Nutcracker—apparently named for the ballet—tend to the trashy side, many sporting such wonders as cake-flavored vodka and white chocolate liqueur. We get it! You're feeling festive. But I prefer the more restrained version in the *Mr. Boston Official Bartender's Guide,* which gets all the creamy sweetness it needs from hazelnut-flavored Frangelico and a bit of amaretto. I leave out the egg white so that the cocktail finishes light.

2½ ounces bourbon

½ ounce Frangelico

¼ ounce amaretto

¼ ounce orgeat syrup

¼ ounce lemon juice

6 to 10 granules kosher salt

Ice cubes

In a cocktail shaker, combine the bourbon, Frangelico, amaretto, orgeat, lemon juice and salt. Shake with ice cubes, then strain into a coupe.

POUR ME ANOTHER

★ NOW TRY ★

Pendennis Club, 69
Orange Martini, 68
Lime in de Coconut, 83
The Fitzroy, 239
Brando Russian, 91
Chai Slide, 92
Dolce Vita, 133
South of the Border, 248
The Porker, 138

DOLCE VITA

Sweet life, indeed! Though various drinks trot about under the name Dolce Vita, the one we care about is a simple blend of bourbon, sweet vermouth and hazelnut liqueur. The result is a rich, lightly nutty Manhattan. I find it also benefits from the balancing brightness a dash of orange bitters brings.

2 ounces bourbon

½ ounce sweet vermouth

¼ ounce Frangelico

⅛ ounce (¾ teaspoon) agave or
   simple syrup

Dash orange bitters

Ice cubes

In a stirring glass, combine the bourbon, sweet vermouth, Frangelico, syrup and bitters. Stir with ice cubes. Strain into a cocktail glass.

POUR ME ANOTHER

★ NOW TRY ★

Vesper, 71
Apple Pie Cocktail, 215
Fish House Punch, 216
Exposition Cocktail, 70
The Fitzroy, 239
Brando Russian, 91
Chai Slide, 92
Nutcracker, 132
The Porker, 138

THE BROWN DERBY

Dale DeGroff credits The Brown Derby—a simple shake of bourbon, grapefruit juice and honey—to the Vendôme Club in Los Angeles back in the 1930s. Around that same time, Harry Craddock was serving up something called a De Rigueur Cocktail, the only difference being the use of Scotch instead of bourbon. I prefer the sweetness—and lack of peat—of the bourbon, so I stayed in that lane for this Whiskey Sour–like cocktail. I've also made this with pineapple juice—crazy good.

2½ ounces bourbon
½ ounce grapefruit juice
¼ ounce honey

6 to 10 granules kosher salt
Ice cubes

In a cocktail shaker, combine the bourbon, grapefruit juice, honey and salt. Shake with ice cubes, then strain into a coupe.

POUR ME ANOTHER
★ NOW TRY ★

Ginger Screw, 101
Piña Colada, 192
Bennett, 44
Knickerbocker, 206
Fedora, 208
Sex on the Beach, 96
Mary Pickford Cocktail, 207
A Slice of Pie, 97
Roman Punch, 205

GRANDFATHER

This seemingly simple cocktail delivers big flavor. Think of it as a fruity Manhattan. The sweetness of the apple brandy and vermouth threaten to push it over the edge, but dashes of both Angostura and Peychaud's bitters keep things on track. If you want to add even more complexity, give the glass an absinthe rinse just before straining the cocktail into it.

2 ounces bourbon

½ ounce apple brandy

½ ounce sweet vermouth

⅛ ounce (¾ teaspoon) agave or
  simple syrup

Dash Angostura bitters

Dash Peychaud's bitters

Ice cubes

In a stirring glass, combine the bourbon, brandy, sweet vermouth, syrup, Angostura bitters and Peychaud's bitters. Stir with ice cubes. Strain into a Nick and Nora glass.

POUR ME ANOTHER
★ NOW TRY ★

Ginger Screw, 101
Improved Screwdriver, 98
Blue Monday Cocktail, 99
Piña Colada, 192
Bennett, 44
Knickerbocker, 206
Fedora, 208
Sex on the Beach, 96
Mary Pickford Cocktail, 207
A Slice of Pie, 97
Roman Punch, 205

DR. B

FRUITY

SWEET

STRONG

As a product of his times, Harry Craddock might get a pass on having chosen an offensive name for this drink. Originally called the Oriental Cocktail, it's a fruity-sweet concoction vaguely reminiscent of a Manhattan, but with bright citrus notes. I'm not sure I buy Craddock's backstory for it. Supposedly, in 1924 an American engineer in the Philippines nearly died but for the medical miracles performed by a mysterious Dr. B. In gratitude, the engineer gifted this recipe to the doctor. Either way, the story at least provides a better name for it.

2 ounces rye

¼ ounce sweet vermouth

¼ ounce orange liqueur

⅛ ounce (¾ teaspoon) agave or
    simple syrup

⅛ ounce (¾ teaspoon) lime juice

6 to 10 granules kosher salt

Ice cubes

In a stirring glass, combine the rye, sweet vermouth, orange liqueur, syrup, lime juice and salt. Stir with ice cubes, then strain into a Nick and Nora glass.

POUR ME ANOTHER

★ NOW TRY ★

Ginger Screw, 101
Improved Screwdriver, 98
Blue Monday Cocktail, 99
Piña Colada, 192
Bennett, 44
Knickerbocker, 206
Fedora, 208
Sex on the Beach, 96
Grandfather, 135
Mr. 404, 100
Mary Pickford Cocktail, 207
A Slice of Pie, 97
Roman Punch, 205

RYE ALGONQUIN

FRUITY

STRONG

CREAMY

Though there is a rum version of the Algonquin, the original is all about the rye and pineapple juice. The two cocktails have little in common beyond an association to the Algonquin Hotel in New York City during the early 1900s. It's surprising how well rye works with pineapple juice, creating a sophisticated, yet lightly tropical vibe. Some liken it to a fruity Whiskey Martini, but I think it's closer in spirit to a Dry Manhattan.

2 ounces rye

1 ounce pineapple juice

½ ounce dry vermouth

⅛ ounce (¾ teaspoon) agave or
   simple syrup

Dash orange bitters

6 to 10 granules kosher salt

Ice cubes

In a cocktail shaker, combine the rye, pineapple juice, dry vermouth, syrup, bitters and salt. Shake with ice cubes, then strain into a cocktail glass.

POUR ME ANOTHER
★ NOW TRY ★

Rum Algonquin, 214
Dry Manhattan, 149

THE PORKER

SWEET
CREAMY
STRONG
(MEATY)

Fat-washing is a clever way of infusing a liquor with the flavor of a fatty ingredient, in this case bacon. Sounds crazy, but it works. The idea is that fatty ingredients contain plenty of alcohol-soluble flavor molecules. Combine them for a while, let those molecules leach out into the liquor, then strain out the fat and you're left with all the flavor, none of the grease. Usually, the process takes a while, but we speed it up by using the freezer to chill and solidify the bacon fat, making it easy to strain away. This bacon-infused bourbon then becomes the base of a seriously indulgent Old Fashioned. And yes, the recipe does call for 3½ ounces of bourbon, but don't worry about the drink being too potent. The fat-washing process inevitably loses a bit of the booze.

1 strip bacon, cut into 1-inch
   pieces
3½ ounces bourbon

½ ounce agave or simple syrup
Dash orange bitters
Ice cubes

In a small skillet over low heat, cook the bacon until lightly crisped, 3 to 5 minutes. Scrape the bacon and any fat in the pan into a 1- or 2-cup glass measuring cup. Add the bourbon. Set aside for 15 minutes. Place the measuring cup in the freezer for another 20 to 30 minutes, or until the fat in the glass is solidifying on top of the bourbon. Line a mesh cocktail strainer with cheesecloth and set it over a stirring glass. Strain the bourbon into the stirring glass; don't press on the solids. Discard the bacon and fat. Add the syrup and bitters to the bourbon, then stir with ice cubes. Strain into a rocks glass with 1 large or 2 standard ice cubes.

POUR ME ANOTHER
★ NOW TRY ★
Lime in de Coconut, 83
Coconut-Lime Daiquiri, 199
The Fitzroy, 239
Jalapeño Yuzu Rumtini, 200
Brando Russian, 91
Chai Slide, 92
Dolce Vita, 133
Nutcracker, 132
South of the Border, 248

THE BIG APPLE

A bit of fresh fruit is a great way to bring out the lighter, brighter side of bourbon. In this case, we muddle slices of fresh apple, which add both flavorful juice and gentle sweetness to the cocktail. Opt for apples with high acidity and lots of flavor, such as Honeycrisp or Macoun.

2 large, thin slices fresh apple
¼ ounce agave or simple syrup
¼ ounce Licor 43
¼ ounce Ancho Reyes

Dash orange bitters
6 to 10 granules kosher salt
Ice, cubes and crushed

In a stirring glass, aggressively muddle the apple slices and syrup. Add the Licor 43, Ancho Reyes, bitters and salt. Stir with ice cubes, then double strain into a coupe filled halfway with crushed ice.

POUR ME ANOTHER
★ NOW TRY ★

A Slice of Pie, 97
Apple Pie Cocktail, 215

THE DERBY

SWEET

FRUITY

REFRESHING

Not to be confused with The Brown Derby cocktail, The Derby combines bourbon, lime juice, sweet vermouth and orange liqueur. But as citrus often can, the lime tends to overwhelm and sour the bourbon. To keep the flavor but lose the sour notes, I use just a lime zest strip. The result is one of those rare refreshing brown cocktails.

1 lime zest strip

2 ounces bourbon

½ ounce sweet vermouth

½ ounce orange liqueur

Dash Angostura bitters

Ice cubes

Rub the lime zest around the rim of a coupe, then add it to the glass. In a cocktail shaker, combine the bourbon, sweet vermouth, orange liqueur and bitters. Shake with ice cubes, then strain into the glass.

POUR ME ANOTHER
★ NOW TRY ★

Gloom Chaser, 220
Crimean Cup à La Marmora, 221
Cossack, 82
Boozy Smoothie, 107
All Jammed Up, 108
Lemon Drop, 117
The Big Apple, 139

WHISKEY SOUR
NO. 2

Though not as common today, most old school Whiskey Sours called for egg white, a flourish that adds a bit of creamy body to the finished cocktail. Trouble is, egg whites need acid to emulsify and I don't like a high-acid Whiskey Sour. So instead, I opt for pineapple juice, which adds gentle acidity and—with vigorous shaking—that frothy viscosity we want.

1 lemon zest strip

3 ounces bourbon

1 ounce pineapple juice

¼ ounce agave or simple syrup

Dash Angostura bitters

Ice cubes

Rub the lemon zest strip around the rim of a coupe, then add it to the glass. In a cocktail shaker, combine the bourbon, pineapple juice, syrup and bitters. Shake without ice. Add ice cubes and shake again. Strain into the glass.

POUR ME ANOTHER

✳ NOW TRY ✳

Whiskey Sour, 163
Rum Old Fashioned, 229

TELL ME
YOU DIDN'T

I did. This is your pumpkin spice latte of cocktails. You're welcome. Be warned: It's stronger than it seems. And keep a close eye on the cider during the final five minutes. As it reduces to a syrup, it can go from thick and delicious to burned and smoking in a flash.

1 cup apple cider

⅛ teaspoon pumpkin pie spice

3 ounces bourbon

Dash chocolate bitters

Dash orange bitters

6 to 10 granules kosher salt

Ice cubes

In a saucepan over low heat, simmer the cider and pumpkin pie spice until thick and reduced to 2 tablespoons, 15 to 20 minutes. Cool completely, then pour into a cocktail shaker (use a silicone spatula to scrape the pan to get all of the syrup). Add the bourbon, chocolate bitters, orange bitters and salt. Shake with ice cubes. Strain into a coupe.

POUR ME ANOTHER
✴ NOW TRY ✴

Bacardí Special Cocktail, 211
Ko Adang, 213
Rum Algonquin, 214
Apple Pie Cocktail, 215
Fish House Punch, 216
The Mule's Hind Leg, 65
Gin Sling, 66

HOOTS MON COCKTAIL

This cocktail's name comes from Scots Gaelic and means something to the effect of, "Hey, man!" Which, OK… By the time Harry Craddock was serving it in London, the drink was a simple blend of Kina Lillet, sweet vermouth and Scotch. Later versions included Angostura bitters. I felt entitled to take some liberties with this and—once I had—was pleasantly surprised by the results. Deceptively smooth and sweet, while still packing a punch.

2 ounces rye

½ ounce sweet vermouth

¼ ounce Lillet Blanc

⅛ ounce (¾ teaspoon) agave or
   simple syrup

Dash orange bitters

Ice cubes

In a stirring glass, combine the rye, sweet vermouth, Lillet Blanc, syrup and bitters. Stir with ice cubes, then strain into a cocktail glass.

POUR ME ANOTHER
★ NOW TRY ★

El Presidente Cocktail, 224
Vodka Special, 110
Loud Speaker, 67
Isla Grande Iced Tea, 261
Ginger Screw, 101
Blue Monday Cocktail, 99
Bennett, 44
Knickerbocker, 206
Fedora, 208
Mary Pickford Cocktail, 207

REMEMBER
THE MAINE

Charles H. Baker Jr. created this feisty pour back in the 1930s, naming it for the USS *Maine*, which sank off the shore of Cuba. Though some people make it with bourbon, the original used rye. The result is reminiscent of a Manhattan, with a nice note of anise from the absinthe. Heering cherry liqueur is the preferred choice, but I use easier-to-source cherry brandy (and a dash of Angostura bitters makes up for the spices the Heering usually adds).

2 ounces rye   **Dash absinthe**
½ ounce sweet vermouth   **Dash Angostura bitters**
¼ ounce cherry brandy   **Ice cubes**

In a stirring glass, combine the rye, sweet vermouth, cherry brandy, absinthe and bitters. Stir with ice cubes, then strain into a Nick and Nora glass.

POUR ME ANOTHER
★ NOW TRY ★

The Last Word, 72
Well-Spoken Russian, 121
1920 Pick-Me-Up, 73
Martinez, 74
Hotel D'Alsace, 145
La Ultima Palabra, 256
Zombie, 231

HOTEL D'ALSACE

SWEET
STRONG
HERBAL

Credit for the brilliant idea of combining resiny rosemary with whiskey goes to David Slape, as recorded in Jim Meehan and Chris Gall's equally brilliant *The PDT Cocktail Book*. Slape's original uses Irish whiskey, which you certainly should try. But I favor the peppery notes of rye. I also tamp down the Bénédictine and orange liqueur to just ¼ ounce each, making them accents to the whiskey, rather than competitors. Do take a gentle hand with the rosemary. It can be potent when muddled too aggressively, so go easy.

2 sprigs fresh rosemary

¼ ounce agave or simple syrup

2 ounces rye

¼ ounce Bénédictine

¼ ounce orange liqueur

Ice cubes

In a cocktail shaker, muddle 1 sprig rosemary and the syrup; leave the muddler in the shaker. Add the rye, Bénédictine and orange liqueur. Swish the muddler to rinse, then remove. Shake with ice cubes, then double strain into a coupe. Garnish with the remaining rosemary sprig.

POUR ME ANOTHER

★ NOW TRY ★

The Last Word, 72
Well-Spoken Russian, 121
1920 Pick-Me-Up, 73
Martinez, 74
Remember the Maine, 144
La Ultima Palabra, 256
Zombie, 231

NARRAGANSETT

Consider this your herbal-forward Manhattan. Deliciously so. The cocktail takes its name from a town in Rhode Island, which in turn takes its name from a Native American tribe. Not sure what—if anything—either has to do with this lovely little sipper. The absinthe in this cocktail replaces the bitters of a traditional Manhattan. But the anise-herbal notes of the absinthe play the same role as the bitters—balancing the sweetness of the bourbon and vermouth. The result is round and full, with plenty of depth.

2 ounces bourbon

1 ounce sweet vermouth

⅛ ounce (¾ teaspoon) absinthe

Ice cubes

In a stirring glass, combine the bourbon, sweet vermouth and absinthe. Stir with ice cubes, then strain into a rocks glass with 1 large or 2 standard ice cubes.

POUR ME ANOTHER
★ NOW TRY ★
The Last Word, 72
Well-Spoken Russian, 121
1920 Pick-Me-Up, 73
Martinez, 74
Remember the Maine, 144
La Ultima Palabra, 256
Zombie, 231

SAN MARTIN COCKTAIL

HERBAL

SWEET

STRONG

David Wondrich dug into the odd history of this drink, which he determined is not named for the sand martin bird (as most people think and sometimes call this). Thanks to its South American origins, he thinks it's instead named for José de San Martín, a leader in South American liberation movements. Classic takes on this cocktail call for gin stirred with sweet vermouth and Green Chartreuse. That's lovely. But lovelier is replacing the gin with bourbon.

2 ounces bourbon

½ ounce sweet vermouth

¼ ounce Green Chartreuse

Ice cubes

In a stirring glass, combine the bourbon, sweet vermouth and Green Chartreuse. Stir with ice cubes, then strain into a cocktail glass.

POUR ME ANOTHER
★ NOW TRY ★

Dry Manhattan, 149
Guadalajara Dos, 270

CHOKER COCKTAIL

Harry Craddock's version of this cocktail calls for whiskey, Pernod and bitters. And, as he says, "no sweetening in any form should be added." He further says, "Drink this and you can drink anything." Not the most encouraging sales pitch. For my version, I opt for the slightly more intense licorice flavor of absinthe over Pernod, but mix as you like. Either way, Craddock used it in a 2:1 ratio of whiskey to Pernod. That might explain his reaction to the finished drink. I tone down the anise notes and add the softening brightness of orange bitters.

2½ ounces bourbon	Dash orange bitters
¼ ounce absinthe	Ice cubes
¼ ounce agave or simple syrup	

In a cocktail shaker, combine the bourbon, absinthe, syrup and bitters. Shake with ice cubes, then strain into a cocktail glass.

POUR ME ANOTHER
★ NOW TRY ★

Cancan, 85
Vodka Martini, 79
French Martini, 104
Vodka Old Fashioned, 124

DRY MANHATTAN

Variations of the Dry Manhattan have been around since at least the early 1900s. The dryness, of course, comes from using dry vermouth rather than the sweet that is typical to the conventional Manhattan (though Harry Craddock, and later Dale DeGroff in his Reverse Manhattan, called for a bit of both dry and sweet in their versions of this cocktail). A strip of lemon zest has been part of the equation since the start, as has the use of both orange and Angostura bitters. The resulting cocktail drinks less like a Manhattan and more like a Bijou (p. 58), a gin drink that is beguilingly reminiscent of an Old Fashioned.

Lemon zest strip

1 maraschino cherry

2½ ounces rye

½ ounce dry vermouth

Dash Angostura bitters

Dash orange bitters

6 to 10 granules kosher salt

Ice cubes

Rub the lemon zest strip around the rim of a cocktail glass, then add it and the cherry to the glass. In a stirring glass, combine the rye, vermouth, both bitters and the salt. Stir with ice cubes, then strain into the glass.

POUR ME ANOTHER

★ NOW TRY ★

Bijou, 58
San Martin Cocktail, 147
Guadalajara Dos, 270

BOULEVARDIER

BITTER
STRONG
SWEET

The Boulevardier is a close cousin of the Negroni, the former pairing whiskey with Campari and sweet vermouth while the latter opts for gin. Most Boulevardiers call for bourbon, but I like the pepperiness of rye, which balances the high-octane blend of sweet, bitter and boozy that is this drink's trademark. The recipe dates to the 1920s, supposedly created by Erskine Gwynne, an American writer living in Paris who founded a magazine called *Boulevardier* —a term that loosely (and appropriately) translates as wealthy, fashionable socialite. Though tradition calls for serving this in a rocks glass, I like to stay true to its name and take it upscale by using a coupe.

2 ounces rye	**6 to 10 granules kosher salt**
½ ounce Campari	**Ice cubes**
½ ounce sweet vermouth	**1 maraschino cherry**

In a stirring glass, combine the rye, Campari, sweet vermouth and salt. Stir with ice cubes, then strain into a coupe. Place the cherry on a cocktail skewer and use it to stir the drink while sipping.

POUR ME ANOTHER
★ NOW TRY ★

Negroni, 61
Jungle Bird, 225

KENTUCKY LONGSHOT

SPICY
STRONG
SWEET

The signature drink of the 1998 Breeders' Cup, the Kentucky Longshot was created by Max Allen Jr., a bartender at Louisville's Seelbach Hotel. His version called for bourbon, a bit of ginger liqueur, a splash of peach brandy and bitters. I decided to give this horse some pep in its step and upped the ginger liqueur and swapped in apricot brandy. The result is a drink with plenty of sweet spice.

2 ounces bourbon
¾ ounce ginger liqueur
¼ ounce apricot brandy

Dash Angostura bitters
Dash orange bitters
Ice cubes

In a cocktail shaker, combine the bourbon, ginger liqueur, apricot brandy and both bitters. Shake with ice cubes, then strain into a cocktail glass.

POUR ME ANOTHER
★ NOW TRY ★
Moscow Mule, 128
Flu Cocktail, 179
Exposition Cocktail, 70
Vesper, 71
Apple Pie Cocktail, 215
Dolce Vita, 133

RUSTY RYE

The Rusty Nail is another one of those cocktails, like the Screwdriver, that has endless aliases depending on the blend of liquors used to make it. The classic is simply Scotch whisky and Drambuie (a liqueur made from Scotch whisky, honey and spices) over ice. Swap bourbon for the Scotch and it becomes a Rusty Bob. Use peat-heavy Islay Scotch whisky and you get a Smoky Nail. And so on. Which brings me to my take on this cocktail, the Rusty Rye. Peppery rye is perfect for balancing the syrupy sweetness of the Drambuie, while just a touch of ginger liqueur brightens everything.

2½ ounces rye
½ ounce Drambuie
¼ ounce ginger liqueur
Dash Angostura bitters

Dash orange bitters
6 to 10 granules kosher salt
Ice, cubes and crushed

In a stirring glass, combine the rye, Drambuie, ginger liqueur, both bitters and salt. Stir with ice cubes, then strain into a coupe filled halfway with crushed ice.

POUR ME ANOTHER
★ NOW TRY ★

Manhattan, 153
Poker Cocktail, 226
Dandy, 156
Vieux Carré, 180

MANHATTAN

There are numerous origin stories for the Manhattan, but all of them place its birth in the late 1800s and in the New York City borough for which it is named. From the start, it has been a simple mix of whiskey (often rye, sometimes bourbon, and during those dark days of Prohibition, Canadian whisky), sweet vermouth and bitters. Somewhere along the line, the maraschino cherry became a must-have, taking the place of the simple syrup sometimes added. With such a simple equation, quality ingredients and proportions are key. This is my answer to that dilemma. I'm generally quite happy with Bulleit rye, Carpano Antica Formula Sweet Vermouth and Luxardo cherries.

2½ ounces rye or bourbon

½ ounce sweet vermouth

2 dashes Angostura bitters

Ice cubes

1 maraschino cherry

In a stirring glass, combine the rye, sweet vermouth and bitters. Stir with ice cubes, then strain into a rocks glass. Add the cherry.

POUR ME ANOTHER
★ NOW TRY ★

Poker Cocktail, 226
Dandy, 156
Vieux Carré, 180
Old Fashioned, 131
Dry Manhattan, 149
Narragansett, 146
Make Your Mark, 76
Martinez, 74

AZTEC'S MARK

Neyah White first crafted the Aztec's Mark at Nopa in San Francisco a couple decades ago, supposedly inspired by Mexican hot chocolate. It's an uncanny blend of flavors that nonetheless works wonderfully. White's version gets its heat from a couple dashes of hot sauce. Go for it if that's all you've got, but I like the more rounded, gentle heat of ¼ ounce of Ancho Reyes.

2 ounces bourbon

½ ounce crème de cacao

¼ ounce Bénédictine

¼ ounce Ancho Reyes

Dash orange bitters

Ice cubes

In a stirring glass, combine the bourbon, crème de cacao, Bénédictine, Ancho Reyes and bitters. Stir with ice cubes, then strain into a cocktail glass.

POUR ME ANOTHER
★ NOW TRY ★

The Mule's Hind Leg, 65
Rum Old Fashioned, 229
Espresso Martini, 123

WHISPER

According to Harry Craddock, the Whisper is a favorite in the West Indies. Or at least it was in his day. The blend of equal parts whiskey, sweet vermouth and dry vermouth puts the result squarely between a Manhattan and a Dry Manhattan. To stand up to the vermouths, I opt for rye. And I favor toning down the ratios to let the whiskey come forward a bit. Craddock also made a similar drink called the Trinity Cocktail that substituted gin for the whiskey.

2 ounces rye

¾ ounce sweet vermouth

¼ ounce dry vermouth

Dash Angostura bitters

Ice cubes

In a stirring glass, combine the rye, sweet vermouth, dry vermouth and bitters. Stir with ice cubes, then strain into a coupe.

POUR ME ANOTHER

★ NOW TRY ★

Gin Sling, 66

Ko Adang, 213

DANDY

The Dandy is a highly aromatic take on the Manhattan, leaning hard into the citrus with strips of both orange and lemon zest. It's amazing how much they can change the character of a drink and a good reminder that we can dramatically influence the flavor of a cocktail without changing the liquid ingredients. Classic versions of this cocktail call for equal parts rye and sweet vermouth (Harry Craddock favored Dubonnet, a similarly spice- and herb-fortified wine), but I prefer to let the vermouth be more of an accent to the whiskey.

1 orange zest strip
1 lemon zest strip
2 ounces rye
½ ounce sweet vermouth
¼ ounce orange liqueur

⅛ ounce (¾ teaspoon) agave or
   simple syrup
Dash Angostura bitters
Ice cubes

One at a time, rub both citrus zest strips around the rim of a cocktail glass, then add them to the glass. In a stirring glass, combine the rye, sweet vermouth, orange liqueur, syrup and bitters. Stir with ice cubes, then strain into the glass.

POUR ME ANOTHER
★ NOW TRY ★

Manhattan, 153
Loud Speaker, 67
Orange Martini, 68

BLOOD AND SAND

Named for the 1922 silent film *Blood and Sand*—starring the "Latin Lover" Rudolph Valentino—and popularized by Harry Craddock a decade later, the Blood and Sand is chaos in a cocktail. Scotch, cherry brandy, sweet vermouth and orange juice. Er… No thanks. But that doesn't mean the drink doesn't have solid bones. To make this concoction a little less crazy, I swap peppery rye in for smoky Scotch, sweeten things up with a bit of agave and— most importantly—retain the brightness of the orange minus the juice by using orange bitters. The result is shockingly good.

2 ounces rye

¼ ounce cherry brandy

¼ ounce sweet vermouth

¼ ounce agave or simple syrup

Dash orange bitters

6 to 10 granules kosher salt

Ice cubes

In a stirring glass, combine the rye, cherry brandy, sweet vermouth, syrup, bitters and salt. Stir with ice cubes, then strain into a cocktail glass.

POUR ME ANOTHER

★ NOW TRY ★

Loud Speaker, 67
Orange Martini, 68
Dandy, 156
Nutcracker, 132

CARRÉ REPRISE

A floral Vieux Carré? The Vieux Carré is my daily sipper, and I like it big and bold—and am dubious about other formulations. Replacing the Bénédictine with elderflower liqueur was the idea of Death & Co mixologist Brian Miller. Despite my initial trepidations, it works wonderfully. Most recipes call for ½ ounce of elderflower, but I think that's a bit too floral. I make up for the lost sweetness with just a hint of syrup.

1 ounce rye

1 ounce cognac

1 ounce sweet vermouth

¼ ounce elderflower liqueur

⅛ ounce (¾ teaspoon) agave or
   simple syrup

Dash Angostura bitters

Dash Peychaud's bitters

Ice cubes

In a stirring glass, combine the rye, cognac, sweet vermouth, elderflower liqueur, syrup, Angostura bitters and Peychaud's bitters. Stir with ice cubes, then strain into a coupe.

POUR ME ANOTHER
★ NOW TRY ★

Vieux Carré, 180
Mexican Vieux Carré, 282
Dandy, 156
Loud Speaker, 67

LINSTEAD COCKTAIL

The original Linstead Cocktail was a shaken blend of Scotch whisky, pineapple juice and Pernod absinthe (or a dash of Pernod bitters in Harry Craddock's version). It's a more anisette-driven take on a cocktail from the same era, the Algonquin, which combines rye, pineapple juice and dry vermouth. My Linstead lands between the two. I favor bourbon's sweetness to rye's peppery bite (and smoky Scotch tends to overwhelm the other flavors), and keep the absinthe to a drop that adds just a hint of herbal flavor.

2½ ounces bourbon

1 ounce pineapple juice

¼ ounce agave or simple syrup

Dash absinthe

6 to 10 granules kosher salt

Ice cubes

In a cocktail shaker, combine the bourbon, pineapple juice, syrup, absinthe and salt. Shake with ice cubes, then strain into a coupe.

POUR ME ANOTHER

★ NOW TRY ★

Loud Speaker, 67
Blood and Sand, 157
Pendennis Club, 69

CHILL IN THE AIR

This is a pared-down and slightly peppery take on Devon Tarby's Ned Ryerson cocktail in *Cocktail Codex*. Where he sweetens with gum syrup and adds complexity via Miracle Mile Castilian bitters, I instead grab ginger liqueur—which does both jobs nicely. The result is exactly the cocktail you need on a cool fall evening.

2 ounces rye
½ ounce apple brandy
½ ounce ginger liqueur

Dash Angostura bitters
Dash orange bitters
Ice cubes

In a stirring glass, combine the rye, apple brandy, ginger liqueur, Angostura bitters and orange bitters. Stir with ice cubes, then strain into a Nick and Nora glass.

POUR ME ANOTHER
★ NOW TRY ★

Linstead Cocktail, 159
Orange Martini, 68
Dandy, 156
Blood and Sand, 157

BULL AND BEAR

STRONG
SWEET

Original recipes for the Bull and Bear, which date to Prohibition, spike bourbon with lime juice, orange liqueur and often grenadine. Lemon juice sometimes stands in for the lime, which I prefer. But as ever, I find citrus tends to overwhelm whiskey. My solution is to flavor the cocktail with a lemon zest strip, which delivers tons of flavor without overpowering the drink the way the juice can.

1 lemon zest strip

2½ ounces bourbon

½ ounce orange liqueur

¼ ounce grenadine

Ice cubes

Rub the lemon zest strip around the rim of a cocktail glass, then add it to the glass. In a stirring glass, combine the bourbon, orange liqueur and grenadine. Stir with ice cubes, then strain into the glass.

POUR ME ANOTHER
★ NOW TRY ★

Exposition Cocktail, 70
Vesper, 71
Apple Pie Cocktail, 215
Dolce Vita, 133

OH, HENRY! COCKTAIL

Harry Craddock is silent on the origins of this Vieux Carré–adjacent cocktail. It has appeared in various forms over the years, sometimes calling for Scotch, sometimes sherry. But I favor Craddock's use of bourbon, which is balanced by herbal-sweet Bénédictine and peppery-sweet ginger liqueur (Craddock calls for ginger ale, but I found that watered down the cocktail too much, while also making it too sweet).

2½ ounces bourbon

¼ ounce Bénédictine

¼ ounce ginger liqueur

Ice cubes

In a stirring glass, combine the bourbon, Bénédictine and ginger liqueur. Stir with ice cubes, then strain into a coupe.

POUR ME ANOTHER

★ NOW TRY ★

Vieux Carré, 180
Exposition Cocktail, 70
Vesper, 71
Bull and Bear, 161

WHISKEY SOUR

The problem with the Whiskey Sour is, well, the sour part. I'm not a fan of lemon juice in whiskey cocktails…pretty much ever. It overpowers the nuances of whiskey with over-the-top sour notes. So my goal with this cocktail was to capture the bright, citrus notes of a proper Whiskey Sour without allowing the drink to succumb to acidity. The solution? Lemon zest and just a drop of lemon juice. The zest adds tons of aromatic notes, which makes us "taste" the lemon with our noses, yet doesn't allow the juice to bully the flavor of the finished cocktail.

1 lemon zest strip

2½ ounces bourbon

¼ ounce agave or simple syrup

Dash lemon juice

6 to 10 granules kosher salt

Ice cubes

Rub the lemon zest strip around the rim of a rocks glass, then add it to the glass. In a cocktail shaker, combine the bourbon, syrup, lemon juice and salt. Shake with ice cubes. Add 1 large or 2 standard ice cubes to the rocks glass, then strain the cocktail into it.

POUR ME ANOTHER
★ NOW TRY ★

Whiskey Sour No. 2, 141
Exposition Cocktail, 70
Vesper, 71
Oh, Henry! Cocktail, 162

BOBBY BURNS

Dating to the early 1900s, the Bobby Burns has gone by various iterations of the name, all of course a reference to the famous Scottish poet. For that reason, Scotch has long been the lead liquor of choice. But too often the smoky notes of Scotch overwhelm a mixed drink. And since the bones of this cocktail are just one step shy of a Vieux Carré (it's missing just the cognac and bitters), I decided to opt for that drink's rye. The Bobby Burns' addition of lemon zest brightens the finished drink without changing the acidity of it.

1 lemon zest strip

2 ounces rye

½ ounce sweet vermouth

½ ounce Bénédictine

Ice cubes

Rub the lemon zest strip around the rim of a Nick and Nora glass, then add it to the glass. In a stirring glass, combine the rye, sweet vermouth and Bénédictine. Stir with ice cubes, then strain into the glass.

POUR ME ANOTHER
★ NOW TRY ★

Brainstorm Cocktail, 171
Vieux Carré, 180
Bijou, 58
Exposition Cocktail, 70

MINT JULEP

Like my Whiskey Sour, my Mint Julep is an attempt to rescue a classic drink from itself, to harness the essence of the cocktail without allowing it to be overwhelmed by its supporting players. In this case, it's the bushel of mint that too often dominates the drink. I wanted the mint to lend its fresh, herbal magic without leaving you feeling victim to bad scratch-and-sniff stickers. The solution was to create an infused sugar syrup, a process that takes just minutes with the help of the microwave. Combined with bourbon and bitters, this syrup delivers everything we want in a Mint Julep without going over the top.

¼ cup loosely packed fresh mint leaves, plus 1 sprig to garnish

½ ounce agave or simple syrup

3 ounces bourbon

Dash Angostura bitters

Ice, cubes and crushed

Roughly chop the mint leaves, then add them to a 1- or 2-cup microwave-safe liquid measuring cup. Add the syrup, then microwave on high for 20 to 30 seconds, or until the syrup bubbles aggressively and the leaves wilt. Set aside for 2 minutes to cool. Use a mesh strainer to strain the syrup into a cocktail shaker, pressing on the leaves to extract as much liquid as possible. Add the bourbon and bitters, then shake with ice cubes. Strain into a coupe filled halfway with crushed ice. Garnish with the mint sprig.

POUR ME ANOTHER

★ NOW TRY ★

Mojito, 186
Mint Fizz, 126

TIPPERARY COCKTAIL NO. 1

STRONG

SWEET
HERBAL

The Tipperary is named for its use of Irish whiskey, which—according to Hugo Ensslin's 1916 recipe—should be mixed in equal parts with sweet vermouth and Green Chartreuse. Later versions of the drink tended to favor a more generous hand with the Irish whiskey. While the Irish whiskey version is delightful and I encourage you to try it, I prefer the more rounded sweetness bourbon lends this cocktail.

2 ounces bourbon
½ ounce sweet vermouth

¼ ounce Green Chartreuse
Ice cubes

In a cocktail shaker, combine the bourbon, sweet vermouth and Green Chartreuse. Shake with ice cubes, then strain into a cocktail glass.

POUR ME ANOTHER
★ NOW TRY ★

Mint Julep, 165
Mojito, 186
Creole Cocktail, 167
Mint Fizz, 126

CREOLE COCKTAIL

STRONG

SWEET
HERBAL

Must everything be reduced to some variation of my favorite cocktail, the Vieux Carré? Yes! The Creole Cocktail has been around since at least the 1930s. And like the Vieux Carré, its origins trace to New Orleans. In the glass, it wonderfully balances the sweetness of the vermouth and Bénédictine with a bitter amaro (in place of the Vieux Carré's cognac). Some early versions also called for maraschino liqueur, but that's overkill. Orange bitters add brightness without further sweetening the cocktail.

2 ounces rye	Dash Fernet-Branca amaro
½ ounce sweet vermouth	Orange bitters
¼ ounce Bénédictine	Ice cubes

In a stirring glass, combine the rye, sweet vermouth, Bénédictine, amaro and bitters. Stir with ice cubes, then strain into a coupe.

POUR ME ANOTHER
✴ NOW TRY ✴

Mint Julep, 165
Mojito, 186
Tipperary Cocktail No. 1, 166
Mint Fizz, 126

PHILLY ASSAULT

STRONG
SWEET
SMOKY
BITTER

This recipe was inspired by a drink at Philadelphia's The Ranstead Room, a classy, moody, sexy speakeasy. This is their bitter take on a basic Manhattan. Bénédictine stands in for the sweet vermouth. But if you like, you can substitute an equal amount of sweet vermouth. It won't have the same herbal complexity, but it will be delicious. The Cynar both sweetens and adds boldly pleasant bitterness. The result is unexpectedly rich and smooth.

2 ounces rye
½ ounce Bénédictine
½ ounce Cynar

3 dashes orange bitters
Ice cubes

In a rocks glass, stir the rye, Bénédictine, Cynar and bitters with 1 large or 2 standard ice cubes.

POUR ME ANOTHER
★ NOW TRY ★
Dolce Vita, 133
Vesper, 71
Bull and Bear, 161
Oh, Henry! Cocktail, 162
Exposition Cocktail, 70

DE LA LOUISIANE

Remove the cognac from a Vieux Carré and you get a De La Louisiane, a drink from 100 years ago in New Orleans and named for Restaurant La Louisiane. The folks at New York's PDT bar serve up a version based on Stanley Clisby Arthur's recipe for it in his 1937 *Famous New Orleans Drinks*. They call for 2 ounces rye to ¾ ounce each sweet vermouth and Bénédictine. But I favor the equal pours of each, as in a true Vieux Carré.

1 ounce rye
1 ounce sweet vermouth
1 ounce Bénédictine
Generous dash absinthe

Generous dash Peychaud's
  bitters
Ice cubes

In a stirring glass, combine the rye, sweet vermouth, Bénédictine, absinthe and bitters. Stir with ice cubes, then strain into a coupe.

POUR ME ANOTHER
★ NOW TRY ★
The Last Word, 72
Well-Spoken Russian, 121
1920 Pick-Me-Up, 73
Martinez, 74
Remember the Maine, 144
Zombie, 231
La Ultima Palabra, 256
Narragansett, 146

WHISKEY COCKTAIL

In the old bartending manuals, there are countless variations of the simple Whiskey Cocktail, many of them iterations of the Old Fashioned. The most interesting version I've found was in William Schmidt's 1891 *The Flowing Bowl: What and When to Drink*. His version adds a hint of absinthe to the mix, which gives the finished cocktail pleasantly anise-herbal notes. Schmidt likes lemon in his cocktail, but I find orange is a better fit. Many Whiskey Cocktails use gum syrup rather than simple syrup, the former containing both sugar and a gum extract that gives a cocktail a pleasant viscosity. Substitute agave or simple syrup if you don't have gum syrup.

1 orange zest strip	2 dashes Angostura bitters
3 ounces bourbon	1 dash absinthe
½ ounce gum syrup	Ice cubes

Rub the orange zest strip around the rim of a rocks glass, then add it to the glass. In a stirring glass, combine the bourbon, gum syrup, bitters and absinthe. Stir with ice cubes, then strain into the rocks glass with 1 large or 2 standard ice cubes.

POUR ME ANOTHER

★ NOW TRY ★

Old Fashioned, 131
Vieux Carré, 180
Improved Whiskey Cocktail, 174
Martinez, 74

BRAINSTORM COCKTAIL

The Brainstorm Cocktail is a close relative of the Bobby Burns, traditionally subbing Irish whiskey for the Scotch, dry vermouth for the sweet vermouth and orange zest for the lemon. I'm often not a fan of dry vermouth in whiskey cocktails (I find the dry, herbal notes generally work better with clear liquors), but in the Brainstorm it works wonderfully. As with the Bobby Burns, I prefer the peppery flavor of rye to Irish whiskey, but you do you.

1 orange zest strip

2 ounces rye

½ ounce Bénédictine

½ ounce dry vermouth

Ice cubes

Rub the orange zest strip around the rim of a Nick and Nora glass, then add it to the glass. In a stirring glass, combine the rye, Bénédictine and dry vermouth. Stir with ice cubes, then strain into the glass.

POUR ME ANOTHER

★ NOW TRY ★

Bobby Burns, 164
Vieux Carré, 180
Bjiou, 58

MONTE CARLO

STRONG

HERBAL

CREAMY

There are a couple ways to look at the Monte Carlo, a drink credited to David Embury back in the 1940s. You could consider it a rye Old Fashioned in which herbal-sweet Bénédictine stands in for the sugar. Or you could consider it a Manhattan in which the Bénédictine subs for the sweet vermouth. Either way, you're left with a cousin of the two that tastes strong and rich and a little sweet and herbal. These days, it typically is served in a rocks glass, but old-school recipes call for a cocktail glass, which I favor.

2½ ounces rye	Ice cubes
½ ounce Bénédictine	Lemon zest twist
Dash Angostura bitters	

In a stirring glass, combine the rye, Bénédictine and bitters. Stir with ice cubes, then strain into a cocktail glass. Garnish with the lemon zest twist.

POUR ME ANOTHER

★ NOW TRY ★

The Last Word, 72
Well-Spoken Russian, 121
1920 Pick-Me-Up, 73
Martinez, 74
Remember the Maine, 144
La Ultima Palabra, 256
Zombie, 231

SOUTHERN (HEMISPHERE) COMFORT

STRONG
_____
HERBAL
CREAMY

This cocktail is loosely inspired by a Harry Craddock classic that's somewhat inappropriately named the Swazi Freeze Cocktail. It was thusly named for its use of Caperitif, a South African vermouth that was popular in his day (and still made today). Apparently, Craddock was unclear on the distinction between South Africa and what then was known as Swaziland, but today is Eswatini. Regardless of the naming issue, my take is a complex, lightly sweet cocktail that straddles the line between Old Fashioned and Manhattan, but with an underlying complexity from the amaro.

2 ounces bourbon
½ ounce apricot brandy
Dash Fernet-Branca amaro

6 to 10 granules kosher salt
Ice cubes

In a cocktail shaker, combine the bourbon, apricot brandy, amaro and salt. Shake with ice cubes, then strain into a coupe.

POUR ME ANOTHER
★ NOW TRY ★
The Last Word, 72
Well-Spoken Russian, 121
1920 Pick-Me-Up, 73
Martinez, 74
Remember the Maine, 144
Zombie, 231
La Ultima Palabra, 256

IMPROVED WHISKEY COCKTAIL

STRONG

HERBAL

FRUITY

There is a whole world of "improved" cocktails, usually classic recipes tarted up a bit. In time, many of these improved versions became classics unto themselves. The Improved Whiskey Cocktail is no exception, it being an iteration of an iteration of an Old Fashioned. So let's start there. Your basic Old Fashioned is whiskey, bitters and sugar. The Fancy-Free substituted maraschino liqueur for the sugar and combined bitters—orange and Angostura. The Improved Whiskey Cocktail built on that with the addition of dashes of absinthe and Peychaud's bitters. My version leans back to the Fancy-Free by keeping the orange bitters, which play so well with the licorice notes of the absinthe. Though typically served in a rocks glass, I up the elegance and pour this boozy number into a cocktail glass.

1 lemon zest strip

2½ ounces bourbon

¼ ounce maraschino liqueur

Dash absinthe

Dash Angostura bitters

Dash orange bitters

Ice cubes

Rub the lemon zest strip around the rim of a cocktail glass, then add it to the glass. In a stirring glass, combine the bourbon, maraschino, absinthe, Angostura bitters and orange bitters. Stir with ice cubes, then strain into the glass.

POUR ME ANOTHER
★ NOW TRY ★

Whiskey Cocktail, 170
Old Fashioned, 131

SAZERAC

STRONG

HERBAL

SWEET

The Sazerac is a classic that has evolved over time. Much of its backstory is presumptive, but most folks agree it was born in New Orleans during the mid- to late-1800s. And it began life as a brandy drink (some suggest that it takes its name from the French cognac Sazerac de Forge et Fils, but other cocktail historians aren't quite convinced) stirred with a bit of sugar and Peychaud's bitters, finished with a squeeze of lemon zest and served in a glass rinsed with absinthe. By the time Harry Craddock got his mitts on it, the Sazerac had made the jump from brandy to rye, and he was happy using either Angostura or Peychaud's bitters. Dale DeGroff favors using both—and I agree—and most current iterations use both cognac and rye.

Splash absinthe

2 ounces rye

½ ounce cognac

¼ ounce agave or simple syrup

Dash Angostura bitters

Dash Peychaud's bitters

Ice cubes

1 lemon zest strip

Pour the absinthe into a Nick and Nora glass, then swirl to coat the inside. Dump out and discard the absinthe. In a stirring glass, combine the rye, cognac, syrup and both bitters. Stir with ice cubes, then strain into the glass. Rub the lemon zest strip around the rim of the glass, then squeeze it over the cocktail and discard.

POUR ME ANOTHER

★ NOW TRY ★

Improved Whiskey Cocktail, 174
The Last Word, 72
Well-Spoken Russian, 121
1920 Pick-Me-Up, 73
La Ultima Palabra, 256
Loaded Pistol, 283
Zombie, 231

BROOKLYN

The Brooklyn is a bittersweet, complex drink that deserves a slow sip. It starts with an ample pour of rye, a bit of dry vermouth and a splash of maraschino liqueur. Traditionally, it also called for Amer Picon, an amaro with orange notes. That's a bit hard to find these days, so I call on a blend of Fernet-Branca amaro and straight up orange liqueur.

2 ounces rye
½ ounce dry vermouth
½ ounce orange liqueur
¼ ounce Fernet-Branca amaro

⅛ ounce (¾ teaspoon)
   maraschino liqueur
Ice cubes

In a stirring glass, combine the rye, dry vermouth, orange liqueur, amaro and maraschino liqueur. Stir with ice cubes, then strain into a cocktail glass.

POUR ME ANOTHER
★ NOW TRY ★
Sazerac, 175
Improved Whiskey Cocktail, 174
The Last Word, 72
Well-Spoken Russian, 121
1920 Pick-Me-Up, 73
La Ultima Palabra, 256
Loaded Pistol, 283
Zombie, 231

ANGEL'S SHARE

Angel's Share is a popular name for whiskey cocktails; you'll find thousands of them parading around, none seemingly related to any of the others. I prefer the one from the *Mr. Boston Official Bartender's Guide,* which calls for a simple blend of bourbon, amaro and crème de cassis with orange bitters. Most other versions put too much emphasis on the amaro; it tends to overwhelm the other ingredients with its bitter notes. My solution is to simply wash the glass with it.

Dash Fernet-Branca amaro   **Dash orange bitters**
2½ ounces bourbon   **Ice cubes**
½ ounce crème de cassis

Pour a generous dash of amaro in a cocktail glass. Swirl the glass to coat the inside, then pour out and discard the amaro. In a stirring glass, combine the bourbon, crème de cassis and bitters. Stir with ice cubes, then strain into the glass.

POUR ME ANOTHER
★ NOW TRY ★

La Rosita, 275
Old Pal, 62
Naked and Famous, 264
Agave Spritz, 276
Hemingway Daiquiri No. 2, 28

KING COLE
COCKTAIL

Classic versions of the King Cole Cocktail date to at least the early 1900s, and most of them garnish the drink with pineapple. I find that at odds with the spicy character of the drink, which is like an Old Fashioned with a kick from amaro. Harry Craddock leaves out the bitters, but many other iterations reliably call for them. I think they help round out the amaro.

3 ounces rye	Dash orange bitters
¼ ounce agave or simple syrup	Dash Peychaud's bitters
⅛ ounce (¾ teaspoon)	Ice, cubes and crushed
Fernet-Branca amaro	

In a stirring glass, combine the rye, syrup, amaro, orange bitters and Peychaud's bitters. Stir with ice cubes, then strain into a coupe filled halfway with crushed ice.

POUR ME ANOTHER
* NOW TRY *

Moscow Mule, 128
Flu Cocktail, 179
Kentucky Longshot, 151

FLU COCKTAIL

STRONG
SPICY

I'm not sure whether Harry Craddock intended the Flu Cocktail to truly cure what ails you, but he nonetheless crafted a delicious drink. His version calls for a combination of ginger extract and ginger brandy married to Canadian whisky. I opt for easier-to-find ginger liqueur and bourbon, the sweet notes of which perfectly balance the drink's peppery bite.

1 lemon zest strip

2½ ounces bourbon

¼ ounce ginger liqueur

⅛ ounce (¾ teaspoon) agave
   or simple syrup

6 to 10 granules kosher salt

Ice cubes

Rub the lemon zest strip around the rim of a Nick and Nora glass, then add it to the glass. In a stirring glass, combine the bourbon, ginger liqueur, syrup and salt. Stir with ice cubes, then strain into the glass.

POUR ME ANOTHER

★ NOW TRY ★

Kentucky Longshot, 151
Moscow Mule, 128
King Cole Cocktail, 178

VIEUX CARRÉ

The Vieux Carré goes back to the 1930s and is named for New Orleans' French Quarter. I was first introduced to it at London's American Bar, when I asked an eager mixologist to give me something reminiscent of an Old Fashioned, but with more happening under the hood. He delivered in spades. The Vieux Carré lives in the deliciously happy space between an Old Fashioned and a Manhattan, sporting gentle sweetness balanced by peppery rye and herbal notes from the Bénédictine. The result is smooth and potent. The recipe has changed little over the years, generally relying on equal parts rye, cognac and sweet vermouth and slightly less Bénédictine, all of it tempered by both Angostura and Peychaud's bitters. Who am I to tinker with perfection?

1 ounce rye

1 ounce cognac

1 ounce sweet vermouth

¾ ounce Bénédictine

Dash Angostura bitters

Dash Peychaud's bitters

Ice cubes

In a stirring glass, combine the rye, cognac, sweet vermouth, Bénédictine and Angostura and Peychaud's bitters. Stir with ice cubes, then strain into a coupe.

POUR ME ANOTHER

★ NOW TRY ★

Manhattan, 153
Mexican Vieux Carré, 282
Carré Reprise, 158

RUM

Rum's natural sweetness lends itself to SOUR and FRUITY drinks. But don't be fooled by rum. That tiki-friendly exterior hides a darker side that easily leans rich and racy. We begin our exploration with the lime-forward DAIQUIRI. Add some mint to that and you go all HERBAL with a MOJITO. From there, it's a short and FRUITY hop to a FOG CUTTER or a MAI TAI. But add some aged rum to the mix and now we are in STRONG and HERBAL ZOMBIE territory. Some sweet vermouth gives us complexion—and complexity— in the POKER COCKTAIL. Finally, toss some lightly sweet bourbon into it and you've got a STRONG, WARM and even CREAMY MISSISSIPPI PUNCH.

When shopping, white rum is straightforward; Bacardí Superior White Rum works in pretty much every cocktail. The world of aged rums, however, is more complicated. They are made pretty much across the world, particularly the Caribbean. Each region has its own style, many of which are great for sipping, and professional mixologists can work wonders with them.

But for the amateurs among us (hand raised!), Caribbean aged rums can be a challenge. Many of them have too prominent a flavor profile, often coming across as bitter or sour in combination with other flavors. The liquors, though lovely, can be difficult to balance in a cocktail.

The winner for me is domestic aged rums, such as Bully Boy Distillers Boston Rum. The clean, yet rich sweetness is perfect for cocktails calling for aged rum. Likewise, rhum agricole has a similarly gentle profile. It's made in the French Caribbean from sugarcane rather than molasses, imparting a cleaner flavor in the finished drink.

Finally, if you are drawn to the flavors of aged Caribbean rums, there is no harm in experimenting with them in these cocktails. I suggest starting by creating custom blends that combine a domestic aged rum with a Caribbean. Tinker with the proportions until you get the combination you like.

DAIQUIRI

The basic Daiquiri is a model of simplicity and balance. Variations date to at least the late 1880s, when Jerry Thomas wrote about a rum sour called the Santa Cruz Sour. But it was during the early 1900s in Havana that the drink became an icon. Constante Ribalaigua Vert at Floradita Bar perfected the blend of white rum, lime juice and sugar. Many classic recipes call for equal parts lime juice and sugar, but I find it too sweet and knock down the sugar just a bit. Bitters aren't common, but I love the lightly herbal-floral notes a dash of Peychaud's bitters adds. If you don't have any, buy some! But Angostura bitters also work well.

3 ounces white rum

½ ounce lime juice

¼ ounce agave or simple syrup

Dash Peychaud's bitters

Ice cubes

In a cocktail shaker, combine the rum, lime juice, syrup and bitters. Shake with ice cubes, then strain into a coupe.

POUR ME ANOTHER

★ NOW TRY ★

Margarita, 235
Vodka Special, 110
Tequila Poncha, 252
Al Pastor Margarita, 262
Bennett, 44
Bee's Knees, 52
Gin Rickey, 53
Salty Dog, 54
Lime in de Coconut, 83
The Brown Derby, 134

ORANGE BAT

REFRESHING

CREAMY

SWEET

FRUITY

As Dale DeGroff pours it, the White Bat is a blend of white rum, Kahlúa, milk or half-and-half, and cola. He had me right up until the cola part. The rest seemed worth playing with. And since everything else in the mix works so well with orange, I decided to lean in on that with both orange liqueur and orange bitters. DeGroff's version is a long drink served with a straw over ice. I opted to make it a blender cocktail. If you're given to this sort of thing, just jam a straw into the blender jar and take it with you. It's that good. And, oddly, the taste is reminiscent of a citrusy root beer.

1½ ounces white rum	Dash orange bitters
1 ounce orange liqueur	6 to 10 granules kosher salt
1 ounce Kahlúa	Ice cubes

In a blender, combine the rum, orange liqueur, Kahlúa, bitters and salt. Add 1 cup ice cubes, then blend until slushy. Pour into a coupe.

POUR ME ANOTHER

★ NOW TRY ★

The Dirty Orange, 64
Hemingway Daiquiri No. 2, 28

BETWEEN
THE SHEETS

Take your basic Sidecar—cognac, orange liqueur and lemon juice—add some white rum and now you have a Between the Sheets, a citrusy, sweet and bright cocktail that packs a punch. Conventional wisdom says it was created by Harry MacElhone of Harry's New York Bar in Paris during the 1930s. It also appears in Harry Craddock's cocktail manual of 1930, so make of that what you will. Traditionally, it was made with a hefty 1 ounce each of the liquors, followed by ¼ ounce of lemon juice. Over the years, many a mixologist found that a bit much, favoring ¾ ounce each of the liquors. Personally, I'm fine with the classic higher-proof pour, but I did want something to tame all that citrus acidity. The answer: Split the rum into ½ ounce each of white and aged, a blend that maintains the overall flavor of the drink, but brings a little complexity to the game.

1 ounce cognac	¼ ounce agave or simple syrup
1 ounce orange liqueur	¼ ounce lemon juice
½ ounce white rum	6 to 10 granules kosher salt
½ ounce aged rum	Ice cubes

In a cocktail shaker, combine the cognac, orange liqueur, both rums, syrup, lemon juice and salt. Shake with ice cubes, then strain into a cocktail glass.

POUR ME ANOTHER

★ NOW TRY ★

Gin Punch, 42
French 75, 30
Bay Breeze, 80
Tiki Tundra, 81
Army and Navy, 29
Opium, 236
Cancan, 85
Vodka Fix, 102
Corpse Reviver, 48
Gin Daisy, 57
Paloma, 255
Navy Grog, 222

MOJITO

REFRESHING
SWEET
HERBAL
SOUR

The Mojito is a close relative of the Daiquiri, adding mint to the latter's basic equation of white rum, lime juice and sugar. And like the Daiquiri, the Mojito came of age in Havana during the first half of the 20th century. In addition to mint, the Mojito also distinguishes itself by being served over crushed ice. Because this ice continues to dilute and chill the drink while it is sipped (and at a faster rate than cubed ice would), I increase the lime juice so the cocktail is bracingly bright and citrusy from start to finish. Limit the amount of ice the cocktail is shaken with as additional insurance against a watered-down drink.

3 sprigs fresh mint
1 ounce lime juice
½ ounce agave or simple syrup

3 ounces white rum
Ice, cubes and crushed

In a cocktail shaker, combine 2 sprigs mint, the juice and syrup, then muddle. Add the rum, then shake with 2 ice cubes. Fill a highball two-thirds with crushed ice. Smack the remaining mint sprig, then add it to the glass. Strain the cocktail into the glass.

POUR ME ANOTHER

★ NOW TRY ★

Tequila Mojito, 269
Vodka Caipirinha, 115
Agua de Tomatillo, 237
Mint Fizz, 126
Mint Julep, 165

DARK AND STORMY

REFRESHING
SWEET

STRONG
SPICY

A true Dark and Stormy—which belongs to the Moscow Mule family—is a blend of dark rum (typically the insanely potent Gosling's Black Seal Bermuda Black Rum) and ginger beer over ice. It has legions of fans, and who am I to tell them they're wrong? But thanks to the heavy, molasses-like boozy notes of the dark rum, I find the whole thing a little medicinal. I wanted a lighter, fruitier version. My solution was switching to aged rum, which lets the peppery ginger beer shine brighter.

1 orange zest strip
Ice cubes
2½ ounces aged rum

2 ounces ginger beer
6 to 10 granules kosher salt

Rub the zest strip around the rim of a rocks glass, then add it to the glass. Add 1 large or 2 standard ice cubes, then add the rum, followed by the ginger beer and salt. Stir gently.

POUR ME ANOTHER
★ NOW TRY ★

Moscow Mule, 128
Singapore Sling, 41

FOG CUTTER

The joke, of course, is that drinking more than one of these potent tiki cocktails doesn't so much cut the fog as it indelibly fogs the mind. With good reason. Credited to Trader Vic Bergeron in the 1940s, the drink has spawned numerous iterations. But all versions pack plenty of citrus, almondy orgeat syrup and as many as five liquors—rum, gin, brandy or cognac, sherry and oftentimes pisco. That's a lot happening. My goal was to keep the complexity, but bring balance to the hodgepodge of flavors happening. Be warned! It is deceptively mild.

2 ounces white rum

1 ounce aged rum

1 ounce orange juice

½ ounce orgeat syrup

½ ounce gin

½ ounce cognac

½ ounce dry sherry

½ ounce pisco

¼ ounce agave or simple syrup

¼ ounce pineapple juice

Dash Angostura bitters

6 to 10 granules kosher salt

Ice cubes

1 sprig fresh mint

1 maraschino cherry

In a cocktail shaker, combine the white rum, aged rum, orange juice, orgeat syrup, gin, cognac, dry sherry, pisco, agave or simple syrup, pineapple juice, bitters and salt. Shake with ice cubes, then strain into a highball with 2 large or 4 to 6 standard ice cubes. Top with the mint and cherry.

POUR ME ANOTHER

★ NOW TRY ★

Moscow Mule, 128
Singapore Sling, 41
Latin Love, 191
Ocean Shore, 49
The Rum and the Restless, 190
Mai Tai, 189

MAI TAI

The Mai Tai is an icon of the tiki cocktail world, leading the charge of fruity, refreshing drinks since it supposedly was created by Trader Vic Bergeron in 1944. I say supposedly because though Bergeron gets all the credit, a version of the drink also appeared in Harry Craddock's 1930 *The Savoy Cocktail Book*. The biggest difference between their versions is Craddock's addition of grenadine. These days bastardizations of this classic tend to be fruity-sugary messes spiked with rum. But the originals got their fruitiness from nothing more than lime juice and orange liqueur. Orgeat syrup—a sugar syrup infused with almonds—is essential for a Mai Tai (and many other tiki cocktails). Though Craddock is silent on the style of rum used in his Mai Tai, Bergeron and everyone after insisted on aged. In fact, he used a 17-year-old bottle. Consider getting the best (oldest) you can. Because this cocktail is served on ample crushed ice, shake it with just a few cubes so it doesn't become too dilute while it is sipped.

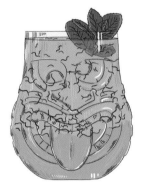

3 ounces aged rum

1 ounce coconut water

¾ ounce lime juice

½ ounce orange liqueur

½ ounce orgeat syrup

Dash Angostura bitters

6 to 10 granules kosher salt

Ice, cubes and crushed

1 sprig fresh mint

In a cocktail shaker, combine the rum, coconut water, lime juice, orange liqueur, orgeat syrup, bitters and salt. Shake with 3 ice cubes, then strain into a rocks glass filled three-quarters with crushed ice. Garnish with the mint sprig.

POUR ME ANOTHER

★ NOW TRY ★

Fog Cutter, 188

Singapore Sling, 41

The Rum and the Restless, 190

Latin Love, 191

Ocean Shore, 49

THE RUM
AND THE RESTLESS

This lesser-known tiki classic is better known as the Restless Native, but I couldn't quite get past those pretty obvious colonialist undertones… So I give you The Rum and the Restless, a refreshing cocktail that blends the brightness of lime with the richness of crème de cacao. The original was made with coconut-flavored rum and a heck of a lot of lime juice. I opt for white rum, the cleaner taste of coconut water and way less lime juice.

2 ounces white rum

1 ounce coconut water

1 ounce crème de cacao

½ ounce lime juice

¼ ounce honey

6 to 10 granules kosher salt

Ice cubes

In a cocktail shaker, combine the rum, coconut water, crème de cacao, lime juice, honey and salt. Shake with ice cubes, then strain into a coupe.

POUR ME ANOTHER
★ NOW TRY ★

Fog Cutter, 188
Singapore Sling, 41
Mai Tai, 189
Ocean Shore, 49

LATIN LOVE

CREAMY

REFRESHING

SWEET

Many cocktails go under this name, and they all tend to lean to the sweet side of the spectrum. Supposedly, this drink was created by Aldo Zegarelli, who used it to win a Most Sensual Cocktail contest sponsored by *Penthouse*. So there's that. The original calls for coconut- and banana-flavored rums, along with pineapple juice, raspberry syrup and sweetened cream of coconut. That's . . . a lot. My version keeps those flavors intact, but cuts the sugar so they can shine. Real banana and coconut milk deliver way more than flavored rums, while also giving this frozen drink some body. The result is frosty, sweet and fruity. And boozy. Don't forget boozy.

3 ounces white rum

1½ ounces coconut milk

1 ounce pineapple juice

2-inch chunk banana

2 teaspoons raspberry jam

¼ ounce agave or simple syrup

6 to 10 granules kosher salt

Ice cubes

In a blender, combine the rum, coconut milk, pineapple juice, banana, jam, syrup and salt. Blend with ¾ cup ice cubes until smooth. Serve in a large coupe or highball.

POUR ME ANOTHER

★ NOW TRY ★

Ocean Shore, 49
Mai Tai, 189
Fog Cutter, 188
Singapore Sling, 41
The Rum and the Restless, 190
Piña Colada, 192

PIÑA COLADA

The Piña Colada is a classic ruined by its popularity. Most iterations are syrupy frozen cocktails weighed down by sugary cream of coconut. Yet the cocktail's origins merit reconsideration. Some say the drink was created by a Puerto Rican pirate in the 1800s as a means of boosting morale for his crew. This seems… dubious. Dave Broom, author of *Rum: The Manual,* offers the more plausible explanation that it grew out of a nonalcoholic pineapple drink in Cuba during the early 1900s. Fast-forward to today and there are countless iterations of the Piña Colada, mostly differentiated by how they source the coconut. Most common is cream of coconut, which is basically sugary coconut fat. Some use coconut cream, which sounds similar but is just the fat of the coconut, no sugar. Others opt for fresh coconut or even coconut sorbet. Most intriguing to me was Harry Craddock's take from 1930, which uses lighter, yet still rich, coconut milk. The resulting cocktail is rich with coconut flavor, but without the cloying weight of so much sugar. Craddock shakes his cocktail and serves it over crushed ice. I was intrigued, but ultimately found the modern convention of using the blender created a better cocktail.

POUR ME ANOTHER

★ NOW TRY ★

Mary Pickford Cocktail, 207
Ocean Shore, 49
Mai Tai, 189
Fog Cutter, 188
The Rum and the Restless, 190
Latin Love, 191
Singapore Sling, 41
Painkiller, 194

2 ounces white rum

1 ounce aged rum

1 ounce pineapple juice

1 ounce coconut milk

½ ounce agave or simple syrup

6 to 10 granules kosher salt

Ice cubes

In a blender, combine the white rum, aged rum, pineapple juice, coconut milk, syrup, salt and 1 cup ice cubes. Blend until smooth, then serve in a generous coupe.

SPICED ORANGE DAIQUIRI

This gently spicy little devil brings heat to the frozen daiquiri game. White rum and vanilla-rich Licor 43 meet up with spicy Ancho Reyes and a bit of orange juice to create the cocktail love child of a Creamsicle and a jalapeño.

2 ounces white rum

1 ounce orange juice

½ ounce Licor 43

½ ounce Ancho Reyes

½ ounce coconut milk

¼ ounce agave or simple syrup

Dash of orange bitters

6 to 10 granules kosher salt

Ice cubes

In a blender, combine the rum, orange juice, Licor 43, Ancho Reyes, coconut milk, syrup, bitters and salt. Blend with 1 cup ice cubes until slushy. Pour into a generous coupe or highball glass.

POUR ME ANOTHER

★ NOW TRY ★

The Poet's Dream, 36
Jungle Bird, 225
Kretchma, 89
The Fitzroy, 239
Toronjil, 241

PAINKILLER

The Painkiller—created during the 1970s at the Soggy Dollar Bar in the British Virgin Islands—is a fruitier take on the Piña Colada. The biggest difference is the addition of orange juice and a finishing sprinkle of nutmeg. Like its cousin, the Painkiller is creamy, frosty and a breeze to pull together in the blender. My version highlights the bright, fruity side by adding orange liqueur and cherry liqueur. But to keep it lighter and avoid an overly sweet cocktail, I use coconut milk instead of the traditional sweetened coconut cream. Aged rum is traditional, but it's also delicious made with white rum.

2½ ounces aged rum

2 ounces coconut milk

½ ounce orange liqueur

½ ounce orange juice

½ ounce pineapple juice

½ ounce agave or simple syrup

¼ ounce maraschino liqueur

Ice cubes

Grated nutmeg

In a blender, combine the rum, coconut milk, orange liqueur, orange juice, pineapple juice, syrup, maraschino liqueur and 1 cup ice cubes. Blend until smooth, then pour into a highball. Top with a sprinkle of nutmeg.

POUR ME ANOTHER

★ NOW TRY ★

Piña Colada, 192
Mary Pickford Cocktail, 207
Ocean Shore, 49
Mai Tai, 189
Fog Cutter, 188
Latin Love, 191
The Rum and the Restless, 190
Singapore Sling, 41
Parisian Blonde, 195

PARISIAN BLONDE

Cream-based cocktails tend to be heavy and palate-deadening. The trick to making them work is ensuring the other flavors are light and bright. In the case of the Parisian Blonde, that role falls to aged rum and ample orange liqueur. The rum adds depth and nuance while the liqueur brings bright, citrusy flavors and sweetness that cuts through the heft of the cream. Traditional recipes call for equal parts rum, orange liqueur and heavy cream. I cut back the cream to give the cocktail a chance to strut its stuff without all that fat. The addition of orange bitters and salt also helps round out and elevate the other flavors.

1¼ ounces orange liqueur

1 ounce aged rum

½ ounce heavy cream

Dash orange bitters

6 to 10 granules kosher salt

Ice cubes

In a cocktail shaker, combine the orange liqueur, rum, cream, bitters and salt. Shake with ice cubes, then strain into a cocktail glass.

POUR ME ANOTHER

★ NOW TRY ★

Buttered Rum, 196
Italian Margarita, 242
Air Mail, 197
A Day at the Beach, 204
Amber on the Rocks, 87
White(-ish) Russian, 88
Guadalajara, 243
Painkiller, 194

BUTTERED RUM

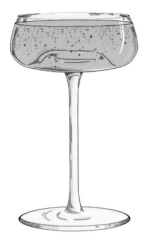

We're turning this one on its head. Traditionally, Buttered Rum is a warm cocktail in which a pat of butter is melted into a heated blend of rum, apple cider and spices. But in my mind, warm cocktails only work in winter. To give this wonderful flavor combination year-round appeal, I borrowed a technique often used with whiskey—fat washing. This involves adding a flavorful fatty ingredient, such as bacon or butter, to a liquor. After a brief infusion, it is chilled so the fat is easily strained out, leaving only its flavor behind. In this case, the result is buttery-rich rum, the perfect foil for bright hard apple cider.

2 ounces aged rum

1 tablespoon melted butter

¼ ounce orange liqueur

¼ ounce agave or simple syrup

Pinch grated nutmeg

Ice cubes

1 ounce hard apple cider

In a small glass, stir together the rum and butter. Let sit for 5 minutes, then place in the freezer for 10 minutes. Line a mesh cocktail strainer with cheesecloth, then pour the butter-rum mixture through it and into a cocktail shaker. Discard the butter. Add the orange liqueur, syrup and nutmeg, then shake with ice cubes. Strain into a coupe, then top with the cider.

POUR ME ANOTHER

★ NOW TRY ★

Parisian Blonde, 195
Italian Margarita, 242
Air Mail, 197
A Day at the Beach, 204
Amber on the Rocks, 87
White(-ish) Russian, 88
Guadalajara, 243
Painkiller, 194

AIR MAIL

The Air Mail is a simple cocktail that is bright, sweet and bubbly. It showed up in the 1949 *Esquire Magazine's Handbook for Hosts* and hasn't changed much since. Honey is the traditional sweetener, but some people use half honey and half simple syrup. I favor the fuller, floral flavor of all honey. And to accent that, I add a dash of orange bitters.

2½ ounces aged rum	6 to 10 granules kosher salt
¼ ounce honey	Ice, cubes and crushed
Dash orange bitters	1 ounce sparkling wine

In a cocktail shaker, combine the rum, honey, bitters and salt. Shake with ice cubes, then strain into a coupe filled halfway with crushed ice. Top with the sparkling wine.

POUR ME ANOTHER

★ NOW TRY ★

Parisian Blonde, 195
Buttered Rum, 242
Italian Margarita, 197
A Day at the Beach, 204
Amber on the Rocks, 87
White(-ish) Russian, 88
Guadalajara, 243
Painkiller, 194

RUM DAISY

CREAMY
SOUR
HERBAL

The basic Daisy is the precursor of the contemporary Margarita (which itself translates as "daisy"). Most recipes consist of some base liquor plus citrus juice and orange liqueur. Over the years, they've been made with pretty much any bottle you care to imagine, but gin, whiskey and rum are the most common. I was particularly intrigued by Robert Vermeire's 1922 take on the Rum Daisy, which offers the substitution of Yellow Chartreuse in place of the orange liqueur, giving the finished cocktail a pleasant herbal sweetness.

2 ounces white rum
½ ounce Yellow Chartreuse
¼ ounce lemon juice

¼ ounce agave or simple syrup
6 to 10 granules kosher salt
Ice cubes

In a cocktail shaker, combine the rum, Yellow Chartreuse, lemon juice, syrup and salt. Shake with ice cubes, then strain into a Nick and Nora glass.

POUR ME ANOTHER
★ NOW TRY ★

Margarita, 235

COCONUT-LIME DAIQUIRI

CREAMY
STRONG

SOUR

This tropical little number was inspired by Vietnamese limeade, which combines ample lime juice with sweetened condensed milk. Since rum loves coconut milk, I substituted that for the sweetened condensed milk, which can be so rich it dulls the other flavors. For another take on this, substitute ½ ounce orange liqueur for an equal amount of the white rum.

3 ounces white rum

1 ounce coconut milk

½ ounce lime juice

½ ounce agave or simple syrup

6 to 10 granules kosher salt

Ice cubes

In a cocktail shaker, combine the white rum, coconut milk, lime juice, syrup and salt. Shake with ice cubes, then strain into a rocks glass with 1 large or 2 standard ice cubes.

POUR ME ANOTHER
★ NOW TRY ★

Lime in de Coconut, 83
The Fitzroy, 239
Jalapeño Yuzu Rumtini, 200
Brando Russian, 91
Chai Slide, 92
Dolce Vita, 133
Nutcracker, 132
South of the Border, 248
The Porker, 138

JALAPEÑO YUZU RUMTINI

Jalapeño? Yuzu? Rum? That's right! This one sounds like a hot mess. Except it somehow isn't. This unusual collection of ingredients comes together in an impressively smooth, creamy drink with just the barest hint of spice. You could, of course, add another jalapeño slice or two if you like the heat. But in this cocktail I prefer it as a subtle background note that plays up the sweet acidity of the yuzu.

1 slice pickled jalapeño
¼ ounce agave or simple syrup
3 ounces white rum

1 ounce sparkling yuzu juice
Ice cubes

In a stirring glass, combine the jalapeño and agave. Muddle, then leaver the muddler in the glass. Add the rum and yuzu juice, then swish the muddler to rinse. Remove the muddler. Gently stir with ice cubes, then double strain into a cocktail glass.

POUR ME ANOTHER
✷ NOW TRY ✷
Spiced Yuzu Margarita, 238
Lime in de Coconut, 83
Dolce Vita, 133
Nutcracker, 132
South of the Border, 248
The Porker, 138

TROPICAL ITCH

At face value, this kitchen sink of a cocktail might seem a bit overwrought. Mango, rum, bourbon, coconut water, orange liqueur... Sure! Why not? Actually, bourbon and rum both pair well with tropical flavors, making them perfect here. My version is loosely based on the drink by Harry Yee, a 1950s pioneer in tropical drinks. I leave out the dark and 151-proof rums that are traditional. I felt they overwhelmed everything else.

2 ounces mango juice

1½ ounces white rum

1 ounce bourbon

1 ounce coconut water

½ ounce orange liqueur

¼ ounce agave or simple syrup

Dash Angostura bitters

6 to 10 granules kosher salt

Ice cubes

In a cocktail shaker, combine the mango juice, rum, bourbon, coconut water, orange liqueur, syrup, bitters and salt. Shake with ice cubes, then strain into a rocks glass with 1 large or 2 standard ice cubes.

POUR ME ANOTHER

★ NOW TRY ★

Gingerberry Pie, 202
Frozen Strawberry Daiquiri, 203
The Poet's Dream, 36
Singapore Sling, 41
Gin Punch, 42

GINGERBERRY PIE

This cocktail has no origin story beyond my love of a chilled slice of blueberry pie topped with ginger ice cream flecked with fresh mint. You with me? It is cool and refreshing and fruity and everything you want on a hot summer night.

2 ounces white rum

1 ounce aged rum

½ ounce ginger liqueur

¼ cup blueberries

2 fresh mint leaves

¼ ounce agave or simple syrup

Dash Angostura bitters

Ice cubes

1 sprig fresh mint, slapped

In a blender, combine the white rum, aged rum, ginger liqueur, blueberries and mint. Pulse several times to finely chop, but not puree, the berries. Let sit for 2 minutes. Double strain into a cocktail shaker, using a spoon to press the solids to extract as much liquid as possible. Add the syrup and bitters. Shake with ice cubes, then strain into a cocktail glass. Garnish with the mint sprig.

POUR ME ANOTHER
★ NOW TRY ★

Mary Pickford Cocktail, 207
Tropical Itch, 201
Ocean Shore, 49
The Rum and the Restless, 190
Mai Tai, 189
Fog Cutter, 188
Latin Love, 191
Singapore Sling, 41

FROZEN STRAWBERRY DAIQUIRI

FRUITY
REFRESHING
SWEET

Despite the chain restaurant vibe it has today, the Strawberry Daiquiri has legit lineage. Like the regular Daiquiri, it is credited to Constante Ribalaigua Vert at Floradita Bar in Havana. His tendency to serve his cocktail on crushed ice caught on just around the same time American cocktail culture took a swing to the sweet. It also wasn't unusual to muddle a few strawberries into the mix. From there, it was a short jump into the blender. Trouble is, over time, the rum got lost behind tons of sugar and too much ice. And don't even get me started about bottled Daiquiri "mixers." Returning this cocktail to the refreshing, fruity classic it once was meant toning down the sugar, controlling the volume of ice and adding dashes of lemon and bitters to balance all the sweet. I could have stopped there, but I loved the gentle vanilla sweetness a bit of Licor 43 added (but if you're a purist, feel free to skip that).

1 cup hulled and quartered strawberries, plus 1 whole	½ ounce agave or simple syrup
2 ounces aged rum	¼ ounce lemon juice
1 ounce white rum	Dash Angostura bitters
½ ounce Licor 43	6 to 10 granules kosher salt
	Ice cubes

In a blender, combine the quartered strawberries, both rums, the Licor 43, syrup, lemon juice, bitters and salt. Add ¾ cup ice cubes. Blend until smooth. Serve in a coupe, then garnish with the whole strawberry on the rim.

POUR ME ANOTHER

★ NOW TRY ★

Not Your Usual Strawberry
Margarita, 253
Mary Pickford Cocktail, 207
Ocean Shore, 49
Singapore Sling, 41
The Rum and the Restless, 190
Mai Tai, 189
Fog Cutter, 188
Latin Love, 191

A DAY AT THE BEACH

The classic A Day at the Beach uses coconut-flavored rum. I prefer the cleaner, more natural flavor of combining white rum with coconut water. The finished cocktail is no less tropical, but tastes brighter and less cloying. The grenadine finish adds both color and fruity sweetness.

2½ ounces white rum

2 ounces coconut water

1 ounce orange juice

1 ounce pineapple juice

½ ounce Amaretto

6 to 10 granules kosher salt

Ice cubes

½ ounce grenadine

In a cocktail shaker, combine the rum, coconut water, orange juice, pineapple juice, Amaretto and salt. Shake with ice cubes, then strain into a highball with 2 large or 4 to 5 standard ice cubes. Slowly pour the grenadine on top.

POUR ME ANOTHER
★ NOW TRY ★

Parisian Blonde, 195
Buttered Rum, 196
Italian Margarita, 242
Air Mail, 197
Amber on the Rocks, 87
White(-ish) Russian, 88
Guadalajara, 243
Painkiller, 194

ROMAN PUNCH

There is a large class of drinks that fall under the category of Rum Punch, and they are the direct ancestors of many of the tiki drinks made popular by Trader Vic's during the second half of the 20th century. But punches as a broader category go back to at least the 17th century and by the end of the 19th century were a staple of the bar world. They typically involve one or more rums, often brandy, sometimes a fruity liqueur, citrus juices and plenty of sweetener. And traditionally they were made in batches to serve a dozen or more people. This is a scaled-down version of a variation known as Roman Punch. It keeps the fruity sweetness, but doesn't let it go overboard. It's nice to be able to actually taste the rum! If you don't have orgeat, an almond-flavored syrup, substitute agave or simple syrup.

2 ounces aged rum

1 ounce cognac

1 ounce orange juice

½ ounce lime juice

¼ ounce orgeat syrup

6 to 10 granules kosher salt

Ice, cubes and crushed

In a cocktail shaker, combine the rum, cognac, orange juice, lime juice, orgeat and salt. Shake with ice cubes, then strain into a coupe filled halfway with crushed ice.

POUR ME ANOTHER

★ NOW TRY ★

Bennett, 44
Fedora, 208
Knickerbocker, 206
Mary Pickford Cocktail, 207
Grandfather, 135
Sex on the Beach, 96
Mr. 404, 100
A Slice of Pie, 97
Improved Screwdriver, 98
Blue Monday Cocktail, 99

KNICKERBOCKER

This fruity blend of aged rum, orange liqueur, raspberry and lemon dates back at least 160 years. It can be served neat, but tradition calls for crushed ice, which is how I like it. While some folks use fresh raspberries, I prefer naturally sweetened raspberry jam. It's easy, adds a gentle sweetness and lends a pleasant viscosity to the finished drink.

2½ ounces aged rum

½ ounce orange liqueur

1 teaspoon raspberry jam

¼ ounce lemon juice

¼ ounce agave or simple syrup

6 to 10 granules kosher salt

Ice, cubes and crushed

In a cocktail shaker, combine the rum, orange liqueur, jam, lemon juice, syrup and salt. Shake with ice cubes, then strain into a coupe filled halfway with crushed ice.

POUR ME ANOTHER
★ NOW TRY ★

Bennett, 44
Fedora, 208
Roman Punch, 205
Mary Pickford Cocktail, 207
Grandfather, 135
Sex on the Beach, 96
Mr. 404, 100
A Slice of Pie, 97
Improved Screwdriver, 98
Blue Monday Cocktail, 99

MARY PICKFORD COCKTAIL

FRUITY
SWEET
CREAMY

Don't believe the many stories that claim this cocktail was named for early 1900s actress Mary Pickford during a trip to Cuba. Historian Cari Beauchamp has thoroughly debunked them. The drink was, however, born in Cuba, where it gained notoriety during Prohibition. Classic recipes called for either equal parts or a 2:1 ratio of pineapple juice to rum, plus a splash of grenadine. They bring its flavor profile close to a Piña Colada, minus the coconut. Over time, maraschino liqueur was added.

2½ ounces white rum
1½ ounces pineapple juice
¼ ounce maraschino liqueur

¼ ounce agave or simple syrup
6 to 10 granules kosher salt
Ice cubes

In a cocktail shaker, combine the rum, pineapple juice, maraschino liqueur, syrup and salt. Shake with ice cubes, then strain into a cocktail glass.

POUR ME ANOTHER

★ NOW TRY ★

Piña Colada, 192
Bennett, 44
Knickerbocker, 206
Fedora, 208
Roman Punch, 205

FEDORA

FRUITY

SWEET

STRONG

The Fedora started life in the late 1800s as a boozy blend of brandy, orange liqueur, aged rum and bourbon, all tarted up with lemon and sugar, then piled with berries and chunks of orange. About 50 years later, William Boothby pared things down by eliminating the fruit cocktail in favor of a single maraschino cherry. That's where we get our starting point for this high-proof cocktail. The earliest recipes called for equal parts brandy and orange liqueur, with only half parts rum and bourbon. I prefer to flip that ratio and let the rum shine.

1 ounce aged rum

¾ ounce bourbon

½ ounce brandy

½ ounce orange liqueur

¼ ounce maraschino cherry syrup (from a jar of maraschino cherries)

Bare squeeze of lemon juice

Ice cubes

In a cocktail shaker, combine the rum, bourbon, brandy, orange liqueur, cherry syrup and lemon juice. Shake with ice cubes, then strain into a cocktail glass.

POUR ME ANOTHER

★ NOW TRY ★

Piña Colada, 192
Bennett, 44
Knickerbocker, 206
Mary Pickford Cocktail, 207
Roman Punch, 205

MARAGATO COCKTAIL

This is a very loosely interpreted cocktail from Harry Craddock. His calls for equal parts rum, sweet vermouth and dry vermouth, plus a dash of cherry liqueur and a whole lot of lemon and lime juice. That was a bit much—and a bit muddled—for me. More contemporary versions, including by Dave Broom and Dale DeGroff, substitute orange juice for the lemon and lime. I took it one step further and eliminated the dry vermouth, which tended to overwhelm the cleaner, sweeter flavors of the other ingredients.

1½ ounces aged rum

½ ounce sweet vermouth

½ ounce orange juice

¼ ounce maraschino liqueur

6 to 10 granules kosher salt

Ice cubes

In a cocktail shaker, combine the rum, sweet vermouth, orange juice, maraschino liqueur and salt. Shake with ice cubes, then strain into a cocktail glass.

POUR ME ANOTHER
★ NOW TRY ★

Vodka Fix, 102

Corpse Reviver, 48

Gin Daisy, 57

Navy Grog, 222

The Monkey Gland, 51

Paloma, 255

SPICY MANGO FROZEN DAIQUIRI

The basic frozen daiquiri offers so many creative directions for alternatives. And I particularly like using frozen fruit instead of ice. The resulting cocktail is frosty and smooth, yet suffers no dilution. This version blends the creamy sweetness of frozen mango with just a hint of spice from a slice of pickled jalapeño. It creates a background note of gentle heat, a nice foil to all the sweet. But if spice doesn't do it for you, leave out the jalapeño.

1½ cups frozen mango chunks	¼ ounce Licor 43
3½ ounces white rum	¼ ounce agave or simple syrup
1 ounce coconut water	1 slice pickled jalapeño
½ ounce orange liqueur	6 to 10 granules kosher salt

In a blender, combine the mango, rum, coconut water, orange liqueur, Licor 43, syrup, jalapeño and salt. Blend until slushy, then pour into a highball.

POUR ME ANOTHER
★ NOW TRY ★

Frozen Strawberry Daiquiri, 203
Not Your Usual Strawberry
Margarita, 253
Mary Pickford Cocktail, 207
Ocean Shore, 49
Mai Tai, 189
The Rum and the Restless, 190
Fog Cutter, 188
Latin Love, 191
Singapore Sling, 41

BACARDÍ SPECIAL COCKTAIL

First, there was the Bacardí Cocktail, a Daiquiri descendant that combines white rum, grenadine and lime juice. Then along came the Bacardí Special Cocktail, a variant that adds gin to the mix. Both, of course, traditionally are made with Bacardí rum (an ingredient choice forced nearly 100 years ago by a lawsuit filed by company executives unhappy that Bacardí Cocktails were being made with off-brand rums). Both versions were hugely popular following the end of Prohibition, particularly in New York City (supposedly thanks to the glowing reviews by *New York World* journalist Karl K. Kitchen). As for which to drink, I'm with Karl. The botanicals of the gin make this a more interesting cocktail.

2 ounces white rum

1 ounce gin

¼ ounce grenadine

¼ ounce lime juice

¼ ounce agave or simple syrup

6 to 10 granules kosher salt

Ice cubes

In a cocktail shaker, combine the rum, gin, grenadine, lime juice, syrup and salt. Shake with ice cubes, then strain into a cocktail glass.

POUR ME ANOTHER

★ NOW TRY ★

QUAKER'S COCKTAIL

FRUITY

STRONG

This blend of rum, brandy, lemon juice and raspberry goes back to at least the 1920s. Traditional recipes call for equal parts rum and brandy, but I up the rum and use cognac instead. I also find it needs a bit of salt and bitters to balance all that sweet. I found the lemon juice overwhelmed the cocktail, but a muddled strip of lemon zest was just right for adding citrusy brightness without sour notes. Finally, raspberry syrup is classic, but I opt for easier—and more flavorful—fresh (or thawed frozen) raspberries muddled along with the lemon zest and agave syrup.

¼ cup fresh raspberries
1 lemon zest strip
¼ ounce agave or simple syrup
2 ounces white rum

1 ounce brandy
Dash Angostura bitters
6 to 10 granules kosher salt
Ice, cubes and crushed

In a cocktail shaker, combine the raspberries, lemon zest strip and syrup. Muddle, then leave the muddler in the shaker. Add the rum, brandy, bitters and salt, then swish the muddler to rinse and remove. Shake with ice cubes, then double strain into a coupe filled halfway with crushed ice.

POUR ME ANOTHER
★ NOW TRY ★

Bacardí Special Cocktail, 211
Ko Adang, 213
Rum Algonquin, 214
Apple Pie Cocktail, 215
Fish House Punch, 216
The Mule's Hind Leg, 65
Gin Sling, 66

KO ADANG

The Ko Adang doesn't seem to exist much outside the pages of the *Mr. Boston Official Bartender's Guide,* but it merits a bit more exposure. The original recipe calls for aged and coconut rums, as well as ginger liqueur, mango nectar, coconut cream and lime juice. It pretty much screams fruity and refreshing. My version loses the coconut rum and coconut cream in favor of the cleaner, more naturally tropical flavor of coconut water.

3 ounces aged rum

2 ounces coconut water

1 ounce mango nectar

¾ ounce ginger liqueur

¼ ounce lime juice

Ice cubes

In a cocktail shaker, combine the rum, coconut water, mango nectar, ginger liqueur and lime juice. Shake with ice cubes, then strain into a rocks glass with 1 large or 2 standard ice cubes.

POUR ME ANOTHER
★ NOW TRY ★

The Mule's Hind Leg, 65
Gin Sling, 66
Bacardí Special Cocktail, 211
Rum Algonquin, 214
Apple Pie Cocktail, 215
Fish House Punch, 216
Quaker's Cocktail, 212

RUM ALGONQUIN

FRUITY
STRONG

HERBAL
SWEET

Several vintage cocktails go by this name, almost all of them connected to the Algonquin Hotel in New York City during the early 1900s. The most common is a mix of rye, dry vermouth and pineapple juice. But Dale DeGroff notes another version first published in Ted Saucier's 1951 *Bottoms Up*. This vaguely Manhattan-esque drink spikes aged rum with herbal Bénédictine. Blackberry liqueur is traditional, but I like maraschino liqueur, which doubles down on the cherry flavor since a syrupy cherry typically is added to the glass.

1 maraschino cherry
2 ounces aged rum
½ ounce Bénédictine
¼ ounce maraschino liqueur

¼ ounce lime juice
¼ ounce agave or simple syrup
Ice cubes

Add the cherry to a rocks glass along with 1 large or 2 standard ice cubes. In a cocktail shaker, combine the rum, Bénédictine, maraschino liqueur, lime juice and syrup. Shake with ice cubes, then strain into the glass.

POUR ME ANOTHER

✶ NOW TRY ✶

Rye Algonquin, 137
The Last Word, 72
Sazerac, 175
Well-Spoken Russian, 121
1920 Pick-Me-Up, 73
La Ultima Palabra, 256

APPLE PIE COCKTAIL

The internet is awash in cocktails named for this dessert, most of them using some combination of apple cider, sugar and spiced rum to approximate its namesake flavor. The results typically aren't the most nuanced thing to grace a cocktail glass. That's why I was intrigued by Harry Craddock's take on it in 1930, presumably an era before the drink-dessert line blurred quite so considerably. His version makes no pretense to mimic apple flavor. Instead, it uses apricot brandy and grenadine to build gentle sweetness on a base of white rum and sweet vermouth. He served his version over crushed ice, but I found this watered it down too much.

2 ounces white rum

½ ounce sweet vermouth

½ ounce apricot brandy

¼ ounce grenadine

6 to 10 granules kosher salt

Ice cubes

In a cocktail shaker, combine the rum, sweet vermouth, brandy, grenadine and salt. Shake with ice cubes, then strain into a coupe.

POUR ME ANOTHER

★ NOW TRY ★

Exposition Cocktail, 70
Vesper, 71
Bacardí Special Cocktail, 211
Ko Adang, 213
Rum Algonquin, 214
Fish House Punch, 216
The Mule's Hind Leg, 65
Gin Sling, 66

FISH HOUSE PUNCH

This fruity, boozy little number goes back to the 1700s, when it was created by Philadelphia's Schuylkill Fishing Company, a gentleman's eating and drinking group. The backbone of this drink—classically made in massive tubs to serve many—is a blend of rum, cognac and peach brandy combined with ample lemon juice and sugar. Since the liquors involved already are quite sweet and bright, I tamed both the lemon and sugar and scaled it down to make a single cocktail.

1½ ounces aged rum

1½ ounces cognac

½ ounce peach brandy

¼ ounce agave or simple syrup

¼ ounce lemon juice

Dash Angostura bitters

6 to 10 granules kosher salt

Ice cubes

In a cocktail shaker, combine the rum, cognac, brandy, syrup, lemon juice, bitters and salt. Shake with ice cubes, then strain into a coupe.

POUR ME ANOTHER

★ NOW TRY ★

Exposition Cocktail, 70
Vesper, 71
Apple Pie Cocktail, 215
Bacardí Special Cocktail, 211
Ko Adang, 213
Rum Algonquin, 214
The Mule's Hind Leg, 65
Gin Sling, 66

SCORPION

Call me antisocial, but I'm not one much for shared bowl-style cocktails. Slurping cheap booze from a communal trough just doesn't do it for me. So my take on the Trader Vic Bergeron classic Scorpion Bowl is to transform it into a single cocktail that retains all the punch of the original. Some recipes favor equal parts rum and gin, but letting the former shine to me seems more appropriate for a tiki drink. The white wine harkens to the original recipes.

2 ounces aged rum

1 ounce cognac

1 ounce dry white wine

1 ounce orange juice

1 ounce orgeat syrup

½ ounce gin

¼ ounce lemon juice

6 to 10 granules kosher salt

Ice cubes

1 sprig fresh mint

1 orange wedge

In a cocktail shaker, combine the rum, cognac, wine, orange juice, orgeat syrup, gin, lemon juice and salt. Shake with ice cubes, then strain into a rocks glass with 1 large or 2 standard ice cubes. Garnish with the mint and orange wedge.

POUR ME ANOTHER

★ NOW TRY ★

Gin Punch, 42
Mai Tai, 189
Singapore Sling, 41
Fog Cutter, 188
The Rum and the Restless, 190
Lemon Drop, 117
Isla Grande Iced Tea, 261

CUBA LIBRE

Here's another entry in the world of cola-based cocktails. Also known as a basic Rum and Coke, the Cuba Libre was first poured in Cuba during the early 1900s just after Coca-Cola became available there. The name—Free Cuba—was a slogan of Cuban independence. By the time Prohibition came around, the drink already was popular in the U.S. The ability of Coke to mask the harsh flavor of bathtub booze solidified its popularity. The classic recipe calls for white rum, Coke and a splash of lime juice, all over ice in a highball. I limit the lime to just the zest; it otherwise tends to taste like that ill-fated soda Coca-Cola with Lime. And to cut the syrupy tendency of this cocktail, I swap the highball for a coupe and serve it with crushed ice. While any cola will work, I like to use cane sugar–sweetened Coca-Cola (usually sold in glass bottles—check the label).

1 lime zest strip	2 ounces Coca-Cola
Crushed ice	Dash Angostura bitters
2 ounces white rum	6 to 10 granules kosher salt

Charro Negro, 284

Rub the zest strip around the rim of a coupe, then add it to the glass. Fill the glass halfway with crushed ice. In a stirring glass, combine the rum, Coke, bitters and salt. Gently stir, then pour into the coupe.

DUNLOP

SWEET

REFRESHING

STRONG

The original Dunlop often is credited to Harry Craddock in the 1930s, but it originated at least a decade before with a different Harry—Harry MacElhone. Those early recipes were little more than sherry, rum and Angostura bitters, sometimes with a bit of sweetener and lime juice. Modern takes on the cocktail swap port for the sherry. I tried them side-by-side and found them equally delicious, the port version having more depth and sweetness. In place of the "punch" sweetener MacElhone calls for, I opt for almond-rich orgeat syrup. You could substitute agave or simple syrup, but you'll lose a little sweet-fruity flavor. I also prefer orange bitters over Angostura; the former adds a brightness the cocktail needs.

2 ounces aged rum

1 ounce dry sherry or tawny port

¼ ounce orgeat syrup

Dash orange bitters

Ice cubes

In a cocktail shaker, combine the rum, sherry or port, orgeat syrup and bitters. Shake with ice cubes, then strain into a cocktail glass.

POUR ME ANOTHER

★ NOW TRY ★

Lemon Drop, 117
Isla Grande Iced Tea, 177
Scorpion, 217

GLOOM CHASER

Gloom apparently made for great cocktail inspiration during the 1920s. Robert Vermeire had one called the Gloom Raiser, which combined gin, grenadine, absinthe and dry vermouth. Sounds a little shaky to me. I prefer Harry MacElhone's Gloom Chaser, which showed up around the same time. His combines two varieties of orange liqueur—Curaçao and Grand Marnier—with grenadine, lemon juice and white rum. Ten years later, Harry Craddock made a cocktail of the same name, but minus the rum. I decided to meet them in the middle, ditching the extraneous orange liqueur, keeping the rum and adding bitters to round out the citrus.

2½ ounces white rum
½ ounce orange liqueur
¼ ounce grenadine
⅛ ounce (¾ teaspoon) lemon
   juice

Dash Angostura bitters
Ice cubes

In a cocktail shaker, combine the rum, orange liqueur, grenadine, lemon juice and bitters. Shake with ice cubes, then strain into a cocktail glass.

POUR ME ANOTHER
★ NOW TRY ★
The Derby, 140
Crimean Cup à La Marmora, 221
Cossack, 82
Boozy Smoothie, 107
All Jammed Up, 108
Lemon Drop, 117
The Big Apple, 139

CRIMEAN CUP
À LA MARMORA

I'd wager this is the only cocktail connected to an Italian general who served in the Crimean War. Jerry Thomas published the recipe for this punch in 1862, his version serving a respectable 30 people. Thomas was inspired by a recipe from Alexis Benoît Soyer, a French chef wildly popular in England during the early 1800s. As the somewhat suspect story goes, the drink is named for Alfonso Ferrero, Cavaliere La Marmora, whose exploits leading the Sardinian army impressed Thomas. My recipe retains the flavors of the original, albeit scaled down a bit.

1 lemon zest strip
2 ounces aged rum
1 ounce cognac
½ ounce orgeat syrup
¼ ounce maraschino liqueur
Ice cubes
1½ ounces sparkling wine

Rub the zest around the rim of a coupe, then add it to the glass. In a cocktail shaker, combine the rum, cognac, orgeat and maraschino liqueur. Strain into the coupe, then top with the sparkling wine.

POUR ME ANOTHER

★ NOW TRY ★

The Derby, 140
Gloom Chaser, 220
Cossack, 82
Boozy Smoothie, 107
All Jammed Up, 108
Lemon Drop, 117
The Big Apple, 139

NAVY GROG

The original grog, introduced to the British Royal Navy back in the 1700s, wasn't much more than hot water, rum, lemon and lime juices, cinnamon and sugar. Jump to the 1950s and Don the Beachcomber turned it into a tiki classic, along the way adding a whole mess of rums, grapefruit juice and bitters. It's a relative of the Zombie, though a slightly less potent one. My version pares things back, letting the rums shine a bit brighter and dialing in the citrus. The result is a refreshing citrus-sweet drink that doesn't hide its rum.

1½ ounces white rum

1½ ounces aged rum

½ ounce honey

½ ounce grapefruit juice

¼ ounce lime juice

Ice cubes

In a cocktail shaker, combine the white rum, aged rum, honey, grapefruit juice and lime juice. Shake with ice cubes, then strain into a coupe.

POUR ME ANOTHER
★ NOW TRY ★

Gin and Tonic, 27

Bee's Knees, 52

Vodka Caipirinha, 115

Cherry-Lime Vodka Rickey, 109

Vodka Gimlet, 118

Bay Breeze, 80

Sex on the Beach, 96

Cosmopolitan, 111

CANADIAN COCKTAIL

SWEET

SOUR

FRUITY
STRONG

Most drinks doing business under the name Canadian Cocktail are a blend of Canadian whisky, sugar and orange liqueur. The cocktail started life made with Jamaica rum. Harry Craddock had several iterations on this theme. His Chinese Cocktail ditches the sugar in favor of grenadine and maraschino liqueur, and adds a splash of Angostura bitters. His Davis Cocktail offers up a dry version that loses most of the sugar in favor of dry vermouth. I liked the simplicity of his basic Canadian, but added the bitters from his Chinese version.

2½ ounces aged rum

¼ ounce orange liqueur

¼ ounce agave or simple syrup

Dash Angostura bitters

6 to 10 granules kosher salt

Ice cubes

In a cocktail shaker, combine the rum, orange liqueur, syrup, bitters and salt. Shake with ice cubes, then strain into a cocktail glass.

POUR ME ANOTHER
★ NOW TRY ★

Bee's Knees, 52
Navy Grog, 222
Vodka Caipirinha, 115
Cherry-Lime Vodka Rickey, 109
Vodka Gimlet, 118
Bay Breeze, 80
Sex on the Beach, 96
Cosmopolitan, 111

EL PRESIDENTE COCKTAIL

There are endless variations of this Havana-born cocktail, supposedly created for Cuba's president during the early 1900s, though which president and by which bartender both remain disputed. At its most simple, El Presidente blends aged rum and dry vermouth along with a bit of orange liqueur and/or grenadine. Over the years, some bartenders swapped sweet vermouth for the dry. Harry Craddock opted to add orange juice, but I prefer Joe and Daniel Schofield's choice of orange bitters for a cleaner citrus flavor.

2 ounces aged rum

½ ounce dry vermouth

½ ounce orange liqueur

⅛ ounce (¾ teaspoon) grenadine

1 dash orange bitters

Ice cubes

In a stirring glass, combine the rum, dry vermouth, orange liqueur, grenadine and bitters. Stir with ice cubes, then strain into a Nick and Nora glass.

POUR ME ANOTHER

★ NOW TRY ★

Inca, 55
Vodka Special, 110
Vodka Gimlet, 118
French Martini, 104

JUNGLE BIRD

SWEET

CREAMY

FRUITY

This modern tiki classic was created by Jeffrey Ong at the Kuala Lumpur Hilton's Aviary Bar in the 1970s. The original is a simple, pleasant combination of dark rum, bittersweet Campari, pineapple and lime juices, and a bit of sugar. To take this drink further along the tiki continuum, I opt for white rum and falernum syrup, an almond-citrus sweetener commonly used in tiki drinks. The result is fruitier and sweeter without leaning too hard in either direction.

2 ounces white rum

½ ounce Campari

½ ounce pineapple juice

¼ ounce falernum syrup

¼ ounce lime juice

Ice cubes

In a cocktail shaker, combine the rum, Campari, pineapple juice, falernum syrup and lime juice. Shake with ice cubes, then strain into a Nick and Nora glass.

POUR ME ANOTHER

★ NOW TRY ★

Negroni, 61
Kretchma, 86
Creamsicle, 105
Spiced Orange Daiquiri, 193

POKER COCKTAIL

The Poker Cocktail is rum's answer to the Manhattan, delivering unexpectedly warm, strong and lightly sweet flavor. Its origins are a bit murky, but it goes back to at least the 1930s, when Harry Craddock includes it without note in *The Savoy Cocktail Book*. Classic versions of the drink often are equal parts white rum and sweet vermouth. I prefer to up the rum and add just a hint of sugar and a dash of bitters, all of which inches the finished cocktail even further along the Manhattan continuum.

2 ounces white rum

1 ounce sweet vermouth

¼ ounce agave or simple syrup

Dash Angostura bitters

Ice cubes

In a cocktail shaker, combine the rum, sweet vermouth, syrup and bitters. Shake with ice cubes, then strain into a rocks glass.

POUR ME ANOTHER

★ NOW TRY ★

Manhattan, 153
Bijou, 58

ONE COOL CUCUMBER

STRONG

REFRESHING

SWEET

The One Cool Cucumber takes its lead from a Gin and Tonic, bringing the cooling flavors of cucumber and mint to that basic equation, and ditching the gin in favor of sweeter, cleaner white rum.

2 thick rounds English cucumber	**3 ounces white rum**
1 sprig fresh mint	**Ice cubes**
¼ ounce agave or simple syrup	**2 ounces tonic water**

In a cocktail shaker, combine the cucumber, mint and syrup. Muddle well, then leave the muddler in the shaker. Add the rum, swish the muddler to rinse, then remove it. Shake with ice cubes. Double strain into a rocks glass with 1 large or 2 standard ice cubes. Top with the tonic water, then gently stir.

POUR ME ANOTHER

★ NOW TRY ★

Gin and Tonic, 27
Hemingway Daiquiri No. 1, 228
Hemingway Daiquiri No. 2, 28
French Martini, 104

HEMINGWAY DAIQUIRI NO. 1

No surprise, but Ernest Hemingway liked a strong Daiquiri. That's why the classic Hemingway Daiquiri—supposedly created for him at El Floridita in Havana around 1930—contains no sugar other than the sweetness of the maraschino liqueur and grapefruit juice. It's good, but it still can come across as simplistically citrusy-sweet. I add a splash of ginger liqueur, which brings bright peppery notes.

2 ounces white rum

½ ounce maraschino liqueur

½ ounce grapefruit juice

¼ ounce lime juice

¼ ounce ginger liqueur

6 to 10 granules kosher salt

Ice cubes

In a cocktail shaker, combine the rum, maraschino liqueur, grapefruit juice, lime juice, ginger liqueur and salt. Shake with ice cubes, then strain into a coupe.

POUR ME ANOTHER

∗ NOW TRY ∗

Hemingway Daiquiri No. 2, 28
French Martini, 194
One Cool Cucumber, 227
Gin and Tonic, 27

RUM OLD FASHIONED

The apparent simplicity of this cocktail doesn't do justice to the depth and nuanced flavors it delivers. The goal was an Old Fashioned suitable for warm weather drinking. A blend of white and aged rums approximates the complexity of bourbon, minus the heft. The combination of orange and chocolate bitters offers both richness and brightness. You're going to want more than one of these.

2½ ounces white rum	Dash orange bitters
½ ounce aged rum	Dash chocolate bitters
¼ ounce agave or simple syrup	Ice cubes

In a stirring glass, combine both rums, the syrup and both bitters. Stir with ice cubes, then strain into a rocks glass with 1 large or 2 standard ice cubes.

POUR ME ANOTHER

★ NOW TRY ★

Old Fashioned, 131
The Mule's Hind Leg, 65
Espresso Martini, 123
Aztec's Mark, 154

KICKER COCKTAIL

The combination of fruity apple brandy and botanical sweet vermouth plays perfectly with the natural sweetness of rum. Harry Craddock christened this combination the Kicker Cocktail, originally calling for two parts rum to one part apple brandy along with a splash of sweet vermouth. I found equal parts rum and brandy played better. A dash of bitters helps balance all that sweetness.

1½ ounces white rum

1½ ounces apple brandy

½ ounce sweet vermouth

¼ ounce agave or simple syrup

Dash Angostura bitters

Ice cubes

In a cocktail shaker, combine the rum, brandy, sweet vermouth, syrup and bitters. Shake with ice cubes, then strain into a cocktail glass.

POUR ME ANOTHER
★ NOW TRY ★

Vesper, 71
Exposition Cocktail, 70
Apple Pie Cocktail, 215
Fish House Punch, 216

ZOMBIE

Though usually credited to Don the Beachcomber, the Zombie's origins also are claimed by many other bartenders and distilleries. Believe what you will, but I tend to side with David Embury, who describes the drink as "an offense against the first principle of drink mixing"—that every ingredient should matter and have a role; don't lard up the ingredient list just because you can. And that does tend to be the way with most Zombie recipes, which often call for at least three rums, plus a profusion of citrus juice and sugar. My goal was to clean this up a bit, preserving its rum-and-fruit-forward personality while also allowing those flavors to shine through. The solution was to pare down to just two rums—white and aged—and use a lighter touch with the juice and sweeteners. I did keep the falernum syrup, which has classic spicy-nutty notes, and cinnamon.

1½ ounces white rum	Bare pinch ground cinnamon
1½ ounces aged rum	Dash Angostura bitters
½ ounce pineapple juice	Dash absinthe
¼ ounce falernum syrup	6 to 10 granules kosher salt
¼ ounce grenadine	Ice, cubes and crushed

In a cocktail shaker, combine both rums, the pineapple juice, falernum syrup, grenadine, cinnamon, bitters, absinthe and salt. Shake with ice cubes, then strain into a highball filled two-thirds with crushed ice.

POUR ME ANOTHER

★ NOW TRY ★

The Last Word, 72
Well-Spoken Russian, 121
1920 Pick-Me-Up, 73
Martinez, 74
Death in the Gulfstream, 56
La Ultima Palabra, 256

MISSISSIPPI PUNCH

STRONG
WARM
CREAMY

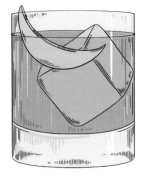

This is another in a long line of rum punch cocktails popular during the 1800s. Unlike the fruity Roman Punch, the Mississippi Punch ditches most of the fruit in favor of the more grownup sweetness of bourbon. In his 1862 *Bartenders Guide,* Jerry Thomas calls for equal parts Jamaica rum and bourbon, plus lemon juice and a whole lot of sugar. I tamed that equation a bit, including reducing the lemon juice to just a zest strip. The result is reminiscent of a Manhattan. So much so, in fact, I added a bit of sweet vermouth to give the cocktail a little roundness.

1 lemon zest strip

2 ounces aged rum

½ ounce bourbon

½ ounce sweet vermouth

¼ ounce agave or simple syrup

6 to 10 granules kosher salt

Ice cubes

Rub the zest strip around the rim of a rocks glass. Add the zest to the glass, then add the rum, bourbon, sweet vermouth, syrup and salt. Stir with 1 large or 2 standard ice cubes.

POUR ME ANOTHER
★ NOW TRY ★

Rum Old Fashioned, 229
Vodka Old Fashioned, 124
Manhattan, 153
Vieux Carré, 180

AGAVE
(TEQUILA AND MEZCAL)

Tequila and mezcal both are made from the agave plant. The biggest difference is that for mezcal, the piña section of the plant is roasted, which accounts for the smoky flavor of the liquor. For tequila, the piña is steamed. The result is two related, but quite different liquors. For comparison, think of mezcal as the Scotch of the whiskey world, while tequila is the bourbon.

Tequila, of course, can be aged. Blanco tequila is unaged. Reposado tequila has been aged up to a year in oak barrels, giving it a slightly smoky richness that places it somewhere between blanco tequila and mezcal in terms of flavor.

All three liquors are used throughout the agave chapter and each can express itself in a variety of ways. Blanco tequila starts with the SWEET and SOUR MARGARITA. It gets CREAMY and tropical when you add coconut water and pineapple juice in THE FITZROY, a drink that brings it closer to a rum tiki drink than a MARGARITA. But by the time you make a CHARRO NEGRO—with a little cola, Ancho Reyes and bitters added in—it's downright STRONG, SPICY and SWEET.

Similarly, the OPIUM shows us the REFRESHING and FRUITY side of mezcal. But it's HERBAL and STRONG in a VENIAL SIN, which includes absinthe, maraschino liqueur and chili bitters. And it struts its assertively STRONG and SMOKY side in LA ROSA, where it is balanced by just hints of orange liqueur and vanilla-spice Licor 43.

While you'll find plenty of premium tequilas, these are best sipped neat or with just a hint of lemon or lime. For both blanco and reposado tequilas, I'm happy with Espolòn. Mezcal options tend to be fewer, but Del Maguey Vida is a solid choice.

A note about sweeteners: Tequila and mezcal have an obvious affinity for agave syrup, so that's my choice in this chapter. But if all you have is simple syrup, by all means use that.

MARGARITA

SWEET

SOUR

FRUITY

REFRESHING

For most of us, this is where tequila begins. Yet the origins of the classic Margarita mostly are lost (and the stories you've heard likely aren't true). What we do know is that it is part of the Daisy family, referring to drinks made from a mix of a liquor, orange liqueur, citrus juice and soda water. Leave out the soda water and you get a Margarita, which translates from the Spanish as "daisy flower."

While there are many creative iterations of the Margarita, two approaches stand out. The classic calls for two parts liquor, one part orange liqueur, and half to three-quarters part citrus juice, the sweetness coming from the liqueur. The other approach, famously created by Tommy's in San Francisco, substitutes a bit of agave syrup for the orange liqueur, the idea being to play the agave backbone of the tequila and sweetener off one another.

I say, why take sides? I prefer my margarita to have a little of both. The high acidity of the cocktail balances all that sweetness, while the orange flavor keeps things light and bright. Finally, the salt. All the flavors at play here love a little salt. But don't put it on the rim of your glass, where it blows out your ability to taste anything else. Instead, add just a few granules to the drink itself to heighten and highlight all the other flavors.

POUR ME ANOTHER

★ NOW TRY ★

Vodka Fix, 102
Daiquiri, 183
Tequila Poncha, 252
Al Pastor Margarita, 262
Smoky Tamarind Margarita, 263
Naked and Famous, 264
Tequila Mojito, 269
Navy Grog, 222

2½ ounces blanco tequila	¼ ounce agave syrup
1 ounce lime juice	6 to 10 granules kosher salt
¾ ounce orange liqueur	Ice cubes

In a cocktail shaker, combine the tequila, lime juice, orange liqueur, syrup and salt. Shake with ice cubes, then strain into a rocks glass with 1 large or 2 standard ice cubes.

OPIUM

This is a reminder that sometimes simple is best. This crisp little number is known as the Opium at Baltra Bar in Mexico City. It's basically a margarita made with mezcal instead of tequila, but the addition of celery bitters nudges it toward the savory side. This also is good with grapefruit juice, creating almost a paloma margarita. Either way, this one sips a little too easy for something so strong.

2½ ounces mezcal

¼ ounce orange liqueur

¼ ounce lemon juice

¼ ounce agave syrup

Dash of celery bitters

6 to 10 granules kosher salt

Ice cubes

In a cocktail shaker, combine the mezcal, orange liqueur, lemon juice, syrup, bitters and salt. Shake with ice cubes, then strain into a coupe.

POUR ME ANOTHER

★ NOW TRY ★

Army and Navy, 29
Bay Breeze, 80
Tiki Tundra, 81
Between the Sheets, 185

AGUA DE TOMATILLO

REFRESHING

HERBAL

SWEET

SOUR

Tomatillos—which resemble small, firm green tomatoes—have a pleasantly sharp-sweet flavor. In Mexico, they often are pureed and combined with lime and mint to create an incredibly refreshing agua fresca–like drink. Though that typically doesn't contain alcohol, the combination is the perfect canvas for a little tequila. Shopping note: If you're unfamiliar with tomatillos, they have a papery husk covering them. Simply peel this off, then rinse the tomatillo to remove the sticky residue.

1 large or 2 medium tomatillos, cut into small pieces

4 ounces blanco tequila

½ ounce lime juice

½ ounce agave syrup

1 sprig fresh mint

6 to 10 granules kosher salt

Ice cubes

In a blender, combine the tomatillos, tequila, lime juice, syrup, mint and salt. Pulse until the tomatillos are finely chopped and have released their juices. Let steep for 2 minutes. Use a mesh strainer to strain into a cocktail shaker, pressing on the solids to extract as much liquid as possible. Discard the solids. Shake with ice cubes. Strain into a coupe.

POUR ME ANOTHER
★ NOW TRY ★

Mojito, 186
Tequila Mojito, 269

SPICED YUZU MARGARITA

REFRESHING
STRONG

Yuzu is an Asian fruit that tastes like a blend of lemon, orange and grapefruit. Which, of course, makes it the perfect companion for citrus-loving tequila. For this simple switch on the margarita, I add Ancho Reyes in place of the usual orange liqueur because the subtle spicy notes balance the sweetness. Sparkling yuzu juice is widely available at larger supermarkets and Asian markets. My favorite brand is Kimino.

2½ ounces blanco tequila

½ ounce Ancho Reyes

¼ ounce agave syrup

6 to 10 granules kosher salt

Ice cubes

1 ounce sparkling yuzu juice

In a cocktail shaker, combine the tequila, Ancho Reyes, syrup and salt. Shake with ice cubes, then strain into a cocktail glass. Top with the sparkling yuzu.

POUR ME ANOTHER
★ NOW TRY ★

Jalapeño Yuzu Rumtini, 200

THE FITZROY

The Fitzroy typically is a Scotch cocktail, often little more than whiskey, sweet vermouth and bitters. Some versions sweeten the deal by adding a splash of rum and simple syrup. My favorite variation, however, is on the menu at Mexico City's Baltra Bar, where tequila stands in for the Scotch, coconut liqueur replaces the rum and—in a move loosely reminiscent of a Piña Colada—everything is married with a bit of horchata, a creamy rice-based drink. It's simply brilliant. For my version, I upped the tequila and opted for lighter coconut water. The horchata was a must, but I leaned into the Piña Colada vibe and added pineapple juice. The result is shockingly good. It's well worth hunting down the horchata powder.

3 ounces blanco tequila

1½ ounces coconut water

¾ ounce pineapple juice

½ ounce orange liqueur

½ teaspoon horchata powder

6 to 10 granules kosher salt

Ice, cubes and crushed

In a cocktail shaker, combine the tequila, coconut water, pineapple juice, orange liqueur, horchata and salt. Shake with ice cubes. Strain into a coupe filled halfway with crushed ice.

POUR ME ANOTHER

★ NOW TRY ★

Jungle Bird, 225
Kretchma, 86
Creamsicle, 105
Spiced Orange Daiquiri, 193

THE UNDERDOG

This cocktail is so named because it really shouldn't work. I was at one of those restaurants where the most redeeming value is the volume of their pours and saw this hot mess of a cocktail on the menu—tequila, amaretto, coconut water and orange juice. I ordered it just to see how bad it was, the cocktail equivalent of rubbernecking. Even the waitress tried to dissuade me from getting it. But I was pleasantly surprised to find the flavors DID work. Remarkably well, in fact. For my version, I doubled down on the almond flavor by using orgeat instead of agave or simple syrup, but that's hardly essential. The result is shockingly creamy and refreshing without feeling heavy.

3 ounces tequila

2 ounces orange juice

1 ounce coconut water

½ ounce amaretto

¼ ounce orgeat syrup

Dash chocolate bitters

6 to 10 granules kosher salt

Ice cubes

In a cocktail shaker, combine the tequila, orange juice, coconut water, amaretto, orgeat, bitters and salt. Shake with ice cubes, then strain into a rocks glass with 1 large or 2 standard ice cubes.

POUR ME ANOTHER

★ NOW TRY ★

Sneaky Sleeper, 95
The Fitzroy, 239
Jungle Bird, 225
Mai Tai, 189
Singapore Sling, 41
Piña Colada, 192

TORONJIL

It never would have occurred to me to pair mezcal and cinnamon, yet both contain smoky, rich notes that complement one another perfectly. It's a lesson I learned at Hotel Casa Awolly in Mexico City, where they take that pairing and keep it fresh with mint and basil, a bit of citrus and floral honey. The result ends up being both creamy and smoky, an unusual—and unusually delicious—combination. Note that the hot water—which helps dissolve the honey—won't result in a warm cocktail.

2 fresh mint leaves

2 fresh basil leaves

½ ounce (3 teaspoons) honey

½ ounce hot water

2½ ounces mezcal

1 ounce orange juice

Pinch ground cinnamon

6 to 10 granules kosher salt

Ice cubes

In a cocktail shaker, combine the mint, basil, honey and hot water. Muddle, then leave the muddler in the shaker. Add the mezcal, orange juice, cinnamon and salt. Swish the muddler to rinse, then remove. Shake with ice cubes. Strain into a coupe.

POUR ME ANOTHER

★ NOW TRY ★

The Root and the Sky, 278
Jungle Bird, 225
Kretchma, 86
The Fitzroy, 239

ITALIAN MARGARITA

The classic margarita calls for four things—tequila, orange liqueur, sugar and lime. This variation, inspired by a cocktail at Bitter & Twisted in Phoenix, keeps the key flavors, but gets to the finish line a little differently. Italian limoncello—a sweet, boldly lemony Italian liqueur—provides most of the sugar and all of the citrus. Coconut water keeps things balanced and adds a bit more natural sweetness. The result is wildly refreshing.

2½ ounces blanco tequila

¾ ounce limoncello

¾ ounce coconut water

¼ ounce agave syrup

6 to 10 granules kosher salt

Ice, cubes and crushed

In a cocktail shaker, combine the tequila, limoncello, coconut water, syrup and salt. Shake with ice cubes, then strain into a coupe filled halfway with crushed ice.

POUR ME ANOTHER
★ NOW TRY ★

Mary Pickford Cocktail, 207
Parisian Blonde, 195
Buttered Rum, 196
Air Mail, 197
A Day at the Beach, 204
Amber on the Rocks, 87
White(-ish) Russian, 88
Guadalajara, 243
Painkiller, 194

GUADALAJARA

All manner of cocktails are called Guadalajara. Most start with blanco tequila, then add citrus, usually orange or lemon, maybe some bitters and often some wine, sometimes sparkling, sometimes fortified. In creating this version, I didn't feel particularly beholden to anything. I ditched the citrus juice in favor of zest, which adds clean flavor without overwhelming the other ingredients with acidity. Mint and chocolate bitters (use mole bitters if you have them) seemed right. And for a punch of heat, just a bit of Ancho Reyes. I found wine of any variety unnecessary. The result is creamy and sweet with a gentle hit of spice.

3-inch strip lime zest
1 sprig fresh mint
¼ ounce agave syrup
2½ ounces blanco tequila

½ ounce Ancho Reyes
Dash chocolate bitters
Ice cubes

In a cocktail shaker, combine the lime zest, mint and syrup. Muddle, then leave the muddler in the shaker. Add the tequila, Ancho Reyes and bitters. Swish the muddler to rinse, then remove. Shake with ice cubes, then double strain into a cocktail glass.

POUR ME ANOTHER
★ NOW TRY ★

Death in the Gulfstream, 56
Parisian Blonde, 195
Buttered Rum, 196
Italian Margarita, 242
Air Mail, 197
A Day at the Beach, 204
Amber on the Rocks, 87
White(-ish) Russian, 88
Painkiller, 194

OLD GEORGE SOUR

Sours typically are little more than liquor, citrus juice and a hint of sugar. But at Baltra Bar in Mexico City, where the liquor of choice is tequila, they give their Sour gusto with hits of absinthe, black pepper and cardamom. Cooling cucumber and creamy egg white keep everything balanced. This is my version of their Old George Sour, a creamy-herbal wonder. The combination may sound odd, but it's insanely good.

2 slices cucumber	½ ounce egg white
¼ ounce agave syrup	¼ ounce absinthe
⅛ teaspoon ground black pepper	¼ ounce lime juice
Pinch ground cardamom	Ice, cubes and crushed
3 ounces reposado tequila	

In a cocktail shaker, combine the cucumber, syrup, black pepper and cardamom. Muddle, then leave the muddler in the shaker. Add the tequila, egg white, absinthe and lime juice. Swish the muddler to rinse, then remove it. Shake with ice cubes, then double strain into a rocks glass filled halfway with crushed ice.

POUR ME ANOTHER

★ NOW TRY ★

Whiskey Sour, 163
Pink Lady, 40

MOLE NEGRO

CREAMY

SPICY

SWEET

The flavors of mole negro—a savory Mexican sauce made from chilies, nuts and a hit of deliciously gritty chocolate—inspired this cocktail. Mezcal is the liquor of choice because its smoky notes pair so perfectly with the bitterness of the chocolate. Cacao nibs offer the perfect balance of sweet and rich, adding chocolate depth without overwhelming sugar. I use the blender to create a speed infusion, delivering big flavor to the mezcal in just minutes.

3 ounces mezcal

1 tablespoon cacao nibs

1 to 2 slices pickled jalapeño

½ ounce orange liqueur

¼ ounce agave syrup

6 to 10 granules kosher salt

Ice, cubes and crushed

In a blender, combine the mezcal, cacao nibs and jalapeño. Pulse until well chopped, but not pureed. Let steep for 2 minutes. Using a mesh cocktail strainer, strain the mezcal into a cocktail shaker. Add the orange liqueur, syrup and salt. Shake with ice cubes, then strain into a coupe filled halfway with crushed ice.

POUR ME ANOTHER
★ NOW TRY ★

Chai Slide, 92

RED SNAPPER

The red pepper jelly in this simple and surprisingly creamy cocktail does triple duty. First, it provides a gentle sweetness. Second, and pretty obviously, it adds a hint of spice. Finally, and less obviously, it gives the finished cocktail a pleasant viscosity. And viscosity—how a cocktail feels in your mouth—is an important but often overlooked part of a great drink. Feel free to play with this cocktail's equation. Mango-pepper jam, pineapple jam or even a straight up jalapeño jelly all would be delicious.

3 ounces reposado tequila   **6 to 10 granules kosher salt**

¼ ounce Licor 43   **Ice, cubes and crushed**

½ tablespoon red pepper jelly

In a cocktail shaker, combine the tequila, Licor 43, jelly and salt. Shake with ice cubes, then double strain into a coupe filled halfway with crushed ice.

POUR ME ANOTHER
★ NOW TRY ★

Jalapeño Yuzu Rumtini, 200

MEZCAL STALK

CREAMY

SMOKY

SWEET

The Mezcal Stalk—a hefty pour of mezcal moderated by orange liqueur, pineapple juice, lemon juice and agave—was created by Joseph Mortera at Limantour bar in Mexico City. But since then, it has been added to menus across the city's bar scene. I had a version at Baltra Bar that added chili-based Ancho Reyes liqueur to the mix, which I thought was pretty special. I followed suit in my version, but ditched the lemon juice, which added too much acidity on top of the pineapple juice.

2½ ounces mezcal

¾ ounce pineapple juice

½ ounce Ancho Reyes

¼ ounce agave syrup

Ice cubes

In a cocktail shaker, combine the mezcal, pineapple juice, Ancho Reyes and syrup. Shake with ice cubes, then strain into a coupe.

POUR ME ANOTHER

★ NOW TRY ★

The Brown Derby, 134

SOUTH OF
THE BORDER

Kahlúa and tequila is not a combination I thought I could get behind. And the South of the Border is one of those cocktails that appears to make little sense. Typically, it is almost equal parts tequila and coffee liqueur, plus a whole lot of lime juice. Not a ton of nuance happening there. But, play with the proportions a bit, and add a bit of kick, then suddenly we have something worth sipping. With the lime juice, the goal is to squeeze just a few drops, so go easy.

2½ ounces reposado tequila

½ ounce Kahlúa

¼ ounce Ancho Reyes

Bare squeeze of juice from
    1 lime wedge

Dash chocolate or mole bitters

6 to 10 granules kosher salt

Ice, cubes and crushed

In a cocktail shaker, combine the tequila, Kahlúa, Ancho Reyes, lime juice, bitters and salt. Shake with ice cubes, then strain into a Nick and Nora glass filled halfway with crushed ice.

POUR ME ANOTHER

★ NOW TRY ★

Buttered Rum, 196
Dolce Vita, 133
Brando Russian, 91
White(-ish) Russian, 88
Nutcracker, 132

MEXICAN
OLD FASHIONED

CREAMY

STRONG

SWEET

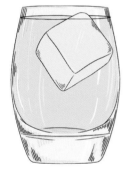

At Limantour, one of Mexico's best bars, richly aged reposado tequila stands in for whiskey in many fresh iterations of classic cocktails. I loved how they used it in their take on the Old Fashioned. And their use of crème de cacao over agave or simple syrup is brilliant, adding depth and richness without weighing down the drink. The orange bitters are my addition, brightening everything and playing so well with the cacao.

2½ ounces reposado tequila	**Dash orange bitters**
½ ounce crème de cacao	**Ice cube**

In a rocks glass, stir the tequila, crème de cacao, bitters and 1 standard ice cube.

POUR ME ANOTHER
★ NOW TRY ★

Old Fashioned, 131
Bijou, 58
Philly Assault, 168

EL DIABLO

El Diablo is tequila's nod to tiki. It first appeared in *Trader Vic's Book of Food and Drink* in 1946. It typically is a highball built in the glass, a combination of ginger ale or ginger beer with tequila, lime juice and soda water topped with a splash of crème de cassis. The latter dribbles down the inside of the glass, creating a purple ombré effect. I find the original a bit lacking, so I upped the tequila, ditched the soda water (which added bubbles, but watered things down) and turned it into a shaken cocktail served over crushed ice.

2½ ounces blanco tequila
½ ounce ginger liqueur
½ ounce crème de cassis

¼ ounce lime juice
Ice, cubes and crushed

In a cocktail shaker, combine the tequila, ginger liqueur, crème de cassis and lime juice. Shake with ice cubes, then strain into a coupe filled halfway with crushed ice.

POUR ME ANOTHER
★ NOW TRY ★

Dark and Stormy, 187

TACUBA COCKTAIL

FRUITY
SWEET

SMOKY

The history of Mexican cuisine is tied tightly to the cooking of monasteries and convents, which were charged with feeding large swaths of the population for many years. So it's only appropriate that one of my favorite cocktails from Mexico City is from Café de Tacuba, a 1912-era restaurant housed in a 17th century convent. Full of stained glass, soaring arched ceilings and a "Room of the Virgins," the restaurant is delightfully trapped in the past; the menu of traditional dishes is mostly unchanged from its earliest years. This is my take on their signature cocktail, which gets bold fruitiness from hibiscus and lime, tempering it with the smoke of mezcal. They served theirs with ample ice, but I prefer it neat.

¼ cup boiling water

1 bag hibiscus tea

1½ ounces agave syrup

3 ounces mezcal

¼ ounce lime juice

6 to 10 granules kosher salt

Ice cubes

In a 1-cup glass measuring cup, combine the water and tea bag. Let steep for 5 minutes. Remove and discard the tea bag, then stir in the syrup. Cool completely. In a cocktail shaker, combine the mezcal, lime juice, hibiscus syrup and salt. Shake with ice cubes, then strain into a coupe.

POUR ME ANOTHER
★ NOW TRY ★

Sneaky Sleeper, 95
Ginger Screw, 101
Improved Screwdriver, 98
Blue Monday Cocktail, 99
Piña Colada, 192
Bennett, 44
Knickerbocker, 206
Fedora, 208
Sex on the Beach, 96
Mary Pickford Cocktail, 207
A Slice of Pie, 97
Roman Punch, 205

TEQUILA PONCHA

The Poncha is a traditional cocktail from the island of Madeira, where it is made using the local (and potent) aguardente de cana, a sugarcane-based liquor that's a relative of cachaça. The cocktail has a reputation as a cold remedy thanks to all the honey and citrus involved. Whatever the truth of those claims, all those flavors also happen to be perfect with tequila.

3 ounces blanco tequila

½ ounce honey

½ ounce orange juice

½ ounce grapefruit juice

¼ ounce lemon juice

Dash Peychaud's bitters

6 to 10 granules kosher salt

Ice cubes

In a cocktail shaker, dry shake the tequila, honey, orange juice, grapefruit juice, lemon juice, bitters and salt. Add ice cubes, then shake again. Strain into a wine glass filled halfway with ice cubes.

POUR ME ANOTHER

★ NOW TRY ★

Pooh Bear, 112
Vodka Special, 110
Daiquiri, 183

NOT YOUR USUAL STRAWBERRY MARGARITA

FRUITY
SWEET
SPICY

Most Strawberry Margaritas—frozen or otherwise—are a shame upon our land. So I set out to discover the sophisticated side of this appealing flavor equation. The solution was to cut the sugar significantly, use fresh fruit (not bottled mixer), add mint for balancing herbal notes, opt for reposado tequila instead of the more typical blanco, and brighten it all with some spicy Ancho Reyes. The result is refreshing and sweet without being saccharine or silly.

2 large strawberries, hulled and
   quartered
1 sprig fresh mint
¼ ounce agave syrup

2½ ounces reposado tequila
½ ounce Ancho Reyes
6 to 10 granules kosher salt
Ice, cubes and crushed

In a cocktail shaker, combine the strawberries, mint and syrup. Muddle. Add the tequila, Ancho Reyes and salt. Shake with ice cubes, then double strain into a coupe filled halfway with crushed ice.

POUR ME ANOTHER
★ NOW TRY ★

Frozen Strawberry Daiquiri, 203
Ginger Screw, 101
Improved Screwdriver, 98
Blue Monday Cocktail, 99
Piña Colada, 192
Bennett, 44
Knickerbocker, 206
Fedora, 208
Sex on the Beach, 96
Mary Pickford Cocktail, 207
A Slice of Pie, 97
Roman Punch, 205
Mr. 404, 100

TEQUILA SUNRISE

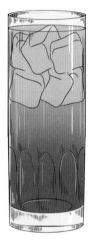

Variations on the Tequila Sunrise are numerous. The original, which little resembles the drinks of today, was born at the Arizona Biltmore Hotel around 1940. At the time, it was a blend of tequila, crème de cassis, lime juice and soda water. Fast-forward about 30 years and the drink got an overhaul by Bobby Lozoff and Billy Rice at the Trident bar in Sausalito, California. A simple highball of unmixed tequila, orange juice and grenadine, the latter slipping to the bottom of the glass and creating the drink's signature ombré effect. Supposedly, the drink was a hit with Mick Jagger, and The Rolling Stones went on to popularize it. For my version, I heat things up with a bit of Ancho Reyes and add some vanilla notes with Licor 43. For even flavor, I do stir those ingredients together, but hew to tradition by adding the grenadine on its own only at the end.

3 ounces orange juice

2½ ounces blanco tequila

½ ounce Ancho Reyes

¼ ounce Licor 43

Ice cubes

1 ounce grenadine

POUR ME ANOTHER

★ NOW TRY ★

The Jaguar, 267

In a stirring glass, combine the orange juice, tequila, Ancho Reyes and Licor 43. Stir without ice. Pour into a highball glass filled three-quarters with ice cubes. Invert a spoon over the glass, pressing it against the inside edge of the glass. Slowly pour the grenadine over it, letting it slide down the inside of the glass and settle to the bottom.

PALOMA

FRUITY

SOUR

SWEET

In Mexico, tequila often is served blended with sweetened sodas, and pretty much anything goes. From Coke (see the Charro Negro, p. 284) to ginger ale to the now famous Squirt, a grapefruit-flavored soda that is the key to the classic Paloma. The recipe itself is almost that simple—just add a squeeze of lime juice. It can be made with either blanco or reposado tequila, or even mezcal. I find that reposado has more of a presence without overwhelming the drink, but have it your way. To me, the real issue is maximizing the grapefruit—threefold! We start with grapefruit juice, which is simmered down to make a thick, intensely flavored syrup. And while bitters aren't traditional in a Paloma, this is a good excuse to hunt down grapefruit bitters. (If you don't have any, substitute orange bitters.) Finally, we keep the finishing splash of grapefruit soda.

½ cup grapefruit juice	Dash grapefruit bitters
3 ounces reposado tequila	6 to 10 granules kosher salt
2 ounces grapefruit soda (such	Ice cubes
as Squirt or Sanpellegrino)	1 lime wedge

In a small saucepan over medium-high heat, simmer the grapefruit juice until reduced by about half. Set aside until cool (to speed the process, pour into a glass measuring cup and place in the freezer for several minutes). Once cool, add the grapefruit syrup to a generous wine glass, then add the tequila, soda, bitters and salt. Stir gently, then add ample ice. Squeeze the lime wedge over the cocktail, then add it.

POUR ME ANOTHER
★ NOW TRY ★

Navy Grog, 222
Vodka Fix, 102
Gin Daisy, 57

LA ULTIMA PALABRA

This agave version of the gin classic The Last Word often is done with either tequila or mezcal; I prefer the smoky notes mezcal brings to the cocktail. Some folks add pineapple juice, but I favor orange liqueur, which better preserves the cleaner lines of the lime and Yellow Chartreuse. Maraschino liqueur is a must.

1½ ounces mezcal

½ ounce Yellow Chartreuse

¼ ounce maraschino liqueur

¼ ounce orange liqueur

¼ ounce lime juice

Dash Angostura bitters

6 to 10 granules kosher salt

Ice cubes

In a cocktail shaker, combine the mezcal, Yellow Chartreuse, maraschino liqueur, orange liqueur, lime juice, bitters and salt. Shake with ice cubes, then strain into a cocktail glass.

POUR ME ANOTHER
★ NOW TRY ★

Well-Spoken Russian, 121
The Last Word, 72

THE RED DEVIL

Tequila loves citrus. It's why so many cocktails with it call for lemon, lime, orange and grapefruit juices. It's the acid that makes the combination work, balancing and brightening the peppery side of the liquor, a little sweetness tying it all together. But they also can overwhelm with sour. So to craft this simple drink, inspired by El Chupacabra, I reached instead for mango juice. It has a more gentle acidity and a more pronounced sweetness. A splash of Campari adds a pleasant bitterness (and sweetness) that brings everything together without getting in the way.

2½ ounces blanco tequila

1 ounce mango juice

½ ounce Campari

Dash Angostura bitters

6 to 10 granules kosher salt

Ice, cubes and crushed

In a cocktail shaker, combine the tequila, juice, Campari, bitters and salt. Shake with ice cubes, then strain into a coupe filled halfway with crushed ice.

POUR ME ANOTHER
★ NOW TRY ★

Spicy Mango Frozen Daiquiri, 210

BURN THE SAGE

The combination of sage and jalapeño gives this otherwise simple cocktail deep herbal-spicy flavor. But the pineapple and tequila keep things light and bright, resulting in a wonderful push-and-pull in the glass.

2 to 4 slices pickled jalapeño
2 fresh sage leaves
¼ ounce agave syrup

3 ounces blanco tequila
1 ounce pineapple juice
Ice, cubes and crushed

In a cocktail shaker, combine the jalapeño, sage and syrup. Muddle, then leave the muddler in the shaker. Add the tequila and pineapple juice, swish the muddler to rinse, then remove it. Shake with ice cubes, then double strain into a rocks glass filled halfway with crushed ice.

POUR ME ANOTHER
★ NOW TRY ★

Spicy Mango Frozen Daiquiri, 210

EL VAMPIRO

Tequila versions of the Bloody Mary abound. In the U.S., they are not-so-cleverly called Bloody Maria. In Mexico, they are known as El Vampiro. However named, most are refreshingly simplified versions of the Bloody Mary, too often an overwrought mess. I've come to prefer the tequila versions; they have a pleasantly smoky-peppery side that complements the tomato. While the Bloody Mary typically is a tall pour served in a highball, I turned this into a sipper served in a coupe. This keeps the ice to a minimum and the flavors bold. I also added a splash of mezcal to up the smoke; it balances the sweeter side of the cocktail.

2 ounces blanco tequila

1 ounce tomato juice

½ ounce mezcal

¼ ounce orange juice

¼ ounce grenadine

¼ teaspoon hot sauce

6 to 10 granules kosher salt

Generous grind black pepper

Ice cubes

In a cocktail shaker, combine the tequila, tomato juice, mezcal, orange juice, grenadine, hot sauce, salt and pepper. Shake with ice cubes, then strain into a coupe.

POUR ME ANOTHER

★ NOW TRY ★

Bloody Mary, 84

MANDARIN TEQUILA CAIPIRINHA

FRUITY

STRONG

REFRESHING

For this boldly citrusy take on tequila, I borrowed the technique of the Caipirinha, muddling the fruit, mint and agave directly in the glass, then adding tequila and ice. I prefer to make this in a jam jar with a tight-fitting lid because I can build the entire thing in the glass, pop on the cover, give it a shake and serve as is. If you prefer, use a cocktail shaker, but don't strain it. Simply pour the entire contents of the shaker into a rocks glass.

1 mandarin orange, cut into quarters
1 sprig fresh mint

¼ ounce agave syrup
3 ounces blanco tequila
Ice cubes

In a jam jar, combine the orange, mint and syrup. Muddle. Add the tequila and ½ cup ice cubes, then put the lid on the jar. Shake well, then remove the lid to serve.

POUR ME ANOTHER

★ NOW TRY ★

Vodka Caipirinha, 115
Bacardí Special Cocktail, 211
Ko Adang, 213
Rum Algonquin, 214
Apple Pie Cocktail, 215
Fish House Punch, 216
The Mule's Hind Leg, 65
Gin Sling, 66

ISLA GRANDE ICED TEA

SWEET

REFRESHING

SMOKY

The classic Long Island Iced Tea usually combines equal parts vodka, gin, tequila, rum and orange liqueur, all married with cola. It's...a lot. Purists will object, but I wanted a tequila-forward version, so I start with a full 2 ounces of reposado tequila, then round out the cocktail with gentle hits of the usual suspects and a bit less cola than is traditional. And while lemon is traditional for this "iced tea," tequila loves lime. The result is a refreshing summer sipper.

2 ounces reposado tequila

¼ ounce vodka

¼ ounce gin

¼ ounce white rum

¼ ounce orange liqueur

¼ ounce lime juice

¼ ounce agave syrup

6 to 10 granules kosher salt

Ice cubes

2 ounces cola

In a stirring glass, combine the tequila, vodka, gin, rum, orange liqueur, lime juice, syrup and salt. Stir without ice. Pour into a highball glass filled with ice cubes. Top with the cola.

POUR ME ANOTHER
★ NOW TRY ★

Long Island Iced Tea, 114
Dunlop, 219

AL PASTOR MARGARITA

SWEET
SOUR
HERBAL
CREAMY

When I first encountered this drink at Limantour bar in Mexico City, I expected the worst. Other patrons told me it tasted like taco seasoning, which brought to mind packets of Old El Paso Taco Seasoning Mix. I was delightfully wrong. The reference is to tacos al pastor, a classic dish in which pork is marinated in chilies, pineapple, herbs and spices. The meat is cooked, then served in tortillas topped with cilantro and lime juice. This drink, created by Limantour's Benjamín Padrón, captures the essence of those flavors, at once tangy, sweet, savory and herbal. It works brilliantly. My version is slightly simpler and leaves out the chili (though feel free to add a pinch of ancho chili powder if you are so inclined).

2 generous sprigs fresh cilantro

2 fresh mint leaves

2 fresh basil leaves

¼ ounce agave syrup

2 ounces blanco tequila

1 ounce pineapple juice

¼ ounce orange liqueur

¼ ounce lime juice

6 to 10 granules kosher salt

Ice cubes

In a cocktail shaker, combine the cilantro, mint, basil and syrup. Muddle, then leave the muddler in the shaker. Add the tequila, pineapple juice, orange liqueur, lime juice and salt. Swish the muddler to rinse it, then remove. Shake with ice cubes, then double strain into a coupe.

POUR ME ANOTHER
★ NOW TRY ★

Toronjil, 241

SMOKY TAMARIND MARGARITA

SWEET

SOUR

FRUITY

SPICY

At swanky restaurant/bar La Capital in Mexico City, fruity-tannic tamarind is paired with smoky mezcal to form the backbone of this pleasantly sweet cocktail. A hit of chili offers heat for balance. Simplifying it for home was mostly about figuring out how to keep the flavor of the tamarind without letting it overwhelm or turn the drink muddy. Bright orange liqueur and lime juice help lighten the load. Tamarind paste is widely available in the supermarket's international aisle, as well as at international markets. And don't be shy with the chili powder. There is plenty of sweetness and acidity, so this drink can handle the heat. And per usual, the salt is best in the drink, not on the rim of the glass. You could dump all the ingredients in a blender and offer this as a slushie-style drink, but I found the flavors and appearance better served over crushed ice.

3 ounces mezcal

½ ounce agave syrup

¼ ounce orange liqueur

¼ ounce lime juice

⅛ teaspoon tamarind paste

Generous pinch ancho chili powder

6 to 10 granules kosher salt

Ice, cubes and crushed

In a cocktail shaker, combine the mezcal, syrup, orange liqueur, lime juice, tamarind, chili powder and salt. Shake with ice cubes. Strain into a coupe filled halfway with crushed ice.

POUR ME ANOTHER

★ NOW TRY ★

Salty Dog, 54

NAKED
AND FAMOUS

Credit for creating the Naked and Famous goes to Joaquín Simó when he was at New York City's Death & Co. His recipe called for equal parts—a bare ¾ ounce—of all ingredients. When I had it at Baltra Bar in Mexico City, those numbers had evolved to 1 ounce each. I enjoyed how the folks at Baltra let the mezcal and Chartreuse come forward a bit, but I cut back the bittersweet Aperol just a hair and way back on the lime, which competed with everything.

1 ounce mezcal

1 ounce Yellow Chartreuse

¾ ounce Aperol

¼ ounce lime juice

Ice cubes

In a cocktail shaker, combine the mezcal, Yellow Chartreuse, Aperol and lime juice. Shake with ice cubes, then strain into a Nick and Nora glass.

POUR ME ANOTHER
★ NOW TRY ★

Vodka Special, 110
Old Pal, 62

BRAVE BULL

This cocktail, a tequila take on the vodka-based Black Russian, supposedly dates to the 1950s. Conventional wisdom holds that it was inspired by the Anthony Quinn movie *The Brave Bulls,* which tells the story of a bullfighter who lost his gumption after an injury. This unusual combination of tequila and Kahlúa has the oomph to rekindle one's nerve. I like mine with a splash of Licor 43 and Ancho Reyes, which add vanilla notes and a bit of heat to perfectly complement the coffee liqueur.

2 ounces blanco tequila	¼ ounce Licor 43
½ ounce Kahlúa	6 to 10 granules kosher salt
½ ounce Ancho Reyes	Ice cubes

In a rocks glass, stir together the tequila, Kahlúa, Ancho Reyes, Licor 43, salt and 3 to 4 standard ice cubes.

POUR ME ANOTHER
★ NOW TRY ★

Brando Russian, 91

AGAVE FUMAR

This simple cocktail uses an unexpected ingredient to double down on mezcal's smoky flavor, and makes a nod to the Spanish influence in Mexico. A tiny pinch of smoked paprika adds sweet-savory smoke to balance out the more peppery notes of the mezcal. The result is a bright and balanced cocktail with pops of lemon and beautiful red flecks.

3 ounces mezcal
¼ ounce agave syrup
¼ ounce lemon juice

Pinch smoked paprika
Ice cubes

In a cocktail shaker, combine the mezcal, syrup, lemon juice and paprika. Shake with ice cubes, then strain into a coupe with 1 large ice cube.

POUR ME ANOTHER
★ NOW TRY ★

El Nopal, 279

THE JAGUAR

SOUR
SWEET

SPICY
SMOKY

This is one of those cocktail recipes that nobody seems to agree on. The classic formulation calls for tequila, Green Chartreuse and Amer Picon, a bittersweet French aperitif. Other versions toss honey, lime and rum into the mix. At Hotel Casa Awolly in Mexico City, the mix was mezcal, Yellow Chartreuse, prickly pear vinegar, sour orange juice and habaneros. All of which is to say, I felt pretty liberated to go my own path on this sour-sweet and lightly spicy-smoky number, but I borrowed inspiration mostly from the folks at Awolly.

2 ounces mezcal

½ ounce Yellow Chartreuse

½ ounce Ancho Reyes

¼ ounce orange juice

⅛ ounce (¾ teaspoon) lime juice

6 to 10 granules kosher salt

Ice cubes

In a cocktail shaker, combine the mezcal, Yellow Chartreuse, Ancho Reyes, orange juice, lime juice and salt. Shake with ice cubes, then double strain into a coupe.

POUR ME ANOTHER
★ NOW TRY ★

Mexican Ginger Beer, 277

COCONUT MARGARITA

SOUR

SWEET

CREAMY

REFRESHING

The world suffers no shortage of banal iterations on the Margarita. Most are little more than too much sugar and fruit, which mask the tequila. This variation stands apart. Borrowing inspiration from the Piña Colada, I pair blanco tequila with naturally—but lightly—sweet coconut water. It gives the drink a refreshing flavor without getting in the way of the other ingredients. The sparkling yuzu juice ties the whole thing together. If you don't have that handy, an equal amount of ginger beer will get you to the finish line.

3 ounces blanco tequila

2 ounces coconut water

¾ ounce lime juice

¼ ounce agave syrup

6 to 10 granules kosher salt

Ice cubes

1 ounce sparkling yuzu juice

In a cocktail shaker, combine the tequila, coconut water, lime juice, syrup and salt. Shake with ice cubes, then strain into a rocks glass. Top with the sparkling yuzu juice.

POUR ME ANOTHER

★ NOW TRY ★

The Root and the Sky, 278

TEQUILA MOJITO

HERBAL

SWEET

SOUR

The mojito is a brilliant drink, in part because the components—the lime, the mint, the hint of sweet—all play so well with rum. They also pair perfectly with the pepperiness of tequila. This play on the basic mojito needs nothing but swapping tequila for the rum—plus a pinch of salt—to be insanely good. To give the tequila even more presence, use reposado tequila.

2 sprigs fresh mint	1 ounce lime juice
½ ounce agave syrup	6 to 10 granules kosher salt
3 ounces blanco tequila	Ice cubes

In a cocktail shaker, combine 1 sprig mint and the syrup. Muddle, then leave the muddler in the shaker. Add the tequila, lime juice and salt, then swish the muddler to rinse it. Shake with ice cubes, then strain into a highball glass filled halfway with ice cubes. Garnish with the remaining sprig of mint.

POUR ME ANOTHER

★ NOW TRY ★

Mojito, 186
Mint Fizz, 126
Mint Julep, 165

GUADALAJARA DOS

Of the many very different concoctions that traipse about under the name Guadalajara, my favorite is this simple blend of tequila, dry vermouth and herbal-sweet Bénédictine. Consider it the smoky-sweet side of the Martini. Garnish with a lemon twist if you like; I prefer it as is. Blanco tequila is standard, but I enjoy the richness of reposado. This is a strong and more herbal take on the basic Guadalajara (p. 243), which throws spicy and sour notes into the mix.

2 ounces reposado tequila
1 ounce dry vermouth

½ ounce Bénédictine
Ice cubes

In a stirring glass, combine the tequila, vermouth and Bénédictine. Stir with ice cubes, then strain into a cocktail glass.

POUR ME ANOTHER
★ NOW TRY ★

Dry Manhattan, 149
San Martin Cocktail, 147

PIEDRA

The Piedra is an old-school Mexican cocktail sipped as much by old men at old bars as it is used to fend off a hangover after a rough night. The classic composition is equal parts blanco tequila, anisette liqueur and fernet. Fernet is an amaro, and in Mexico the bottle of choice typically is Fernet-Vallet, which is boldly herbal and spicy. It can be hard to find in the U.S. So my version, which dials back the fernet and anisette to allow the tequila to shine, opts for easier-to-find Fernet-Branca.

2 ounces blanco tequila

½ ounce Fernet-Branca amaro

¼ ounce anisette liqueur

Ice cubes

In a cocktail shaker, combine the tequila, Fernet-Branca and anisette. Shake with ice cubes, then strain into a Nick and Nora glass.

POUR ME ANOTHER
★ NOW TRY ★

Brooklyn, 176

THE BIRD

At Chapulín restaurant in Mexico City, this fruity-herbal cocktail is served with mezcal, creating a smoky backdrop for the piney rosemary and gin. But getting just the right mezcal was essential to pulling off this balancing act—a big ask for the home bartender. I get more reliably delicious results by using tequila, which delivers the spice of the agave without overwhelming smoke.

2 sprigs fresh rosemary

1 teaspoon raspberry jam

¼ ounce lime juice

2½ ounces blanco tequila

½ ounce gin

¼ ounce agave syrup

6 to 10 granules kosher salt

Ice, cubes and crushed

In a cocktail shaker, combine 1 sprig rosemary, the raspberry jam and lime juice. Muddle, then leave the muddler in the shaker. Add the tequila, gin, syrup and salt. Swish the muddler to rinse; remove the muddler. Shake with ice cubes. Double strain into a rocks glass filled halfway with crushed ice. Garnish with the remaining rosemary sprig.

POUR ME ANOTHER
★ NOW TRY ★

Hotel D'Alsace, 145
Loud Speaker, 67
Orange Martini, 68

ROARING '50S

This cocktail was inspired by a creation of Declan McGurk of American Bar in London (though it came to me by way of Bitter & Twisted in Phoenix). At face value, it has a lot going on. And before I sipped it, it seemed like too much. But the flavors somehow become cohesive, creating a drink reminiscent of an Old Fashioned without sacrificing its distinctive tequila backbone. McGurk uses sweet vermouth, where I opt for lighter, but still sweet Cocchi Americano, which adds a floral fruitiness.

2 ounces reposado tequila

½ ounce Cocchi Americano

½ ounce Cynar

¼ ounce grenadine

Dash absinthe

Ice cubes

In a cocktail shaker, combine the tequila, Cocchi Americano, Cynar, grenadine and absinthe. Shake with ice cubes, then strain into a rocks glass with 2 standard or 1 large ice cube.

POUR ME ANOTHER
★ NOW TRY ★

Martinez, 74
Bull and Bear, 161

VENIAL SIN

The origins of this one are a bit muddled. The cocktail itself is anything but. Clean, herbal and strong with a pop of spice, this is a great drink that demands your attention. It typically is made with Yellow Chartreuse, but I favor a hit of absinthe. The anise notes of the latter help balance the floral-fruitiness of the maraschino and elderflower liqueurs. The chili bitters add a lovely background of heat. If you don't have any, a drop of hot sauce works fine.

1½ ounces reposado tequila

½ ounce mezcal

¼ ounce absinthe

¼ ounce maraschino liqueur

¼ ounce elderflower liqueur

1 to 2 drops chili bitters

Ice cubes

In a stirring glass, combine the tequila, mezcal, absinthe, maraschino liqueur, elderflower liqueur and bitters. Stir with ice cubes, then strain into a cocktail glass.

POUR ME ANOTHER

★ NOW TRY ★

Harvey Wallbanger, 103
Roaring '50s, 273

LA ROSITA

La Rosita essentially is a tequila-based Negroni. Most people agree it first showed up in print during the late 1980s. Credit for popularizing it after that goes to Gary "gaz" Regan, who included a version of it in his 1991 *The Bartender's Bible*. However it came to be, most versions call for earthy reposado tequila cut with dry and sweet vermouths, as well as bittersweet Campari and a dash of Angostura bitters. I like to take the richness up a bit with a combination of orange and chocolate bitters.

2 ounces reposado tequila	**Dash orange bitters**
½ ounce Campari	**Dash chocolate bitters**
½ ounce sweet vermouth	**6 to 10 granules kosher salt**
½ ounce dry vermouth	**Ice cubes**

In a stirring glass, combine the tequila, Campari, sweet vermouth, dry vermouth, orange bitters, chocolate bitters and salt. Stir with ice cubes, then strain into a rocks glass with 1 large or 2 standard ice cubes.

POUR ME ANOTHER
★ NOW TRY ★

Negroni, 61

AGAVE SPRITZ

The classic Aperol Spritz is little more than bittersweet Aperol, sparkling wine and a slice of orange. It's strongly floral-citrusy, a combination that also happens to pair perfectly with tequila. So for this iteration, we craft a boozy summer sipper with plenty of ice and bubbles. Be sure to use reposado tequila for this one. Blanco tequila doesn't have enough presence in the glass to stand up to the other flavors.

2 ounces reposado tequila   **Ice cubes**
1 ounce Aperol   **2 ounces sparkling wine**
Dash orange bitters   **1 slice orange**

In a wine glass, combine the tequila, Aperol and bitters. Stir. Add enough ice to fill the glass about two-thirds. Top with sparkling wine and add the orange slice.

POUR ME ANOTHER
★ NOW TRY ★

Old Pal, 62

MEXICAN GINGER BEER

SPICY
SMOKY
FRUITY
SWEET

In the West African country of Liberia, ginger beer is a simple and refreshing nonalcoholic drink made by steeping fresh ginger with pineapple and citrus juices, usually lemon and lime. Sometimes it's sweetened with molasses, spiked with ground cloves and/or allowed to ferment overnight. The ginger gives it an impressively peppery flavor. The inspiration to turn that into a cocktail came from Natalia Garza, a friend in Mexico who loves to infuse mezcal with all manner of fruits. She encouraged me to try mezcal with fresh ginger, saying the two get along fantastically. She was right. And so was born this snappy little number.

2-inch chunk fresh ginger	**¼ ounce lemon juice**
3 ounces mezcal	**Pinch ground cloves**
2 ounces pineapple juice	**6 to 10 granules kosher salt**
½ ounce agave syrup	**Dash Angostura bitters**
½ ounce lime juice	**Ice, cubes and crushed**

In a blender, combine the ginger, mezcal, pineapple juice, syrup, lime juice, lemon juice, cloves, salt and bitters. Pulse until the ginger is finely chopped but not pureed, about 5 seconds. Let steep for 2 minutes. Strain through a mesh strainer into a cocktail shaker. Shake with ice cubes, then strain into a coupe filled halfway with crushed ice.

POUR ME ANOTHER

★ NOW TRY ★

Dark and Stormy, 187
The Jaguar, 267
Tequila Sunrise, 254

THE ROOT
AND THE SKY

SMOKY
FRUITY

SWEET
REFRESHING

Welcome to the savory, smoky side of the Piña Colada. Mezcal stands in for the rum, while a tiny bit of fresh onion—yes, onion—balances the sweetness of the usual coconut and pineapple. A full ounce of Ancho Reyes adds a spicy hit that keeps things real. Don't fear—the onion won't taste oniony. It adds an aromatic note that is alluringly savory.

½ tablespoon chopped red onion

¼ ounce agave syrup

3 ounces mezcal

1 ounce Ancho Reyes

1 ounce coconut water

1 ounce pineapple juice

6 to 10 granules kosher salt

Ice cubes

In a cocktail shaker, combine the onion and syrup. Muddle, then leave the muddler in the shaker. Add the mezcal, Ancho Reyes, coconut water, pineapple juice and salt. Swish the muddler to rinse, then remove it. Shake with ice cubes, then double strain into a highball glass filled halfway with ice cubes.

POUR ME ANOTHER
★ NOW TRY ★

Tiki Tundra, 81
Dark and Stormy, 187
The Jaguar, 267
Tequila Sunrise, 254

EL NOPAL

At Josefina López Méndez's sleekly modern Chapulín restaurant in Mexico City, El Nopal is a smoky-sweet blend of mezcal, agave syrup, apricot liqueur and lime juice. The smoky mezcal does a wonderful job keeping the sweet and acidic notes grounded. This is my version of that drink, which I thought benefited from a hit of spice, too.

2½ ounces mezcal

1 ounce apricot brandy

¼ ounce agave syrup

¼ ounce lime juice

Generous pinch ancho chili powder

6 to 10 granules kosher salt

Ice, cubes and crushed

In a cocktail shaker, combine the mezcal, apricot brandy, syrup, lime juice, chili powder and salt. Shake with ice cubes, then strain into a rocks glass filled halfway with crushed ice.

POUR ME ANOTHER
★ NOW TRY ★

The Root and the Sky, 278

VICUÑA

SMOKY

SWEET

STRONG

This unusual combination of mezcal and pisco comes from Limantour, one of Mexico's top bars. When you get it there, smoked pineapple and nutmeg bring perfect balance to the sweet pisco and pineapple juice and underscore the smoky traits of the mezcal. Since most of us don't have smoked pineapple handy, I swapped in a bare dash of Liquid Smoke, which is made from smoke-infused water. The resulting cocktail allows the smoke to be center stage, but rounds everything out with gentle acidity and sweetness, plus a hint of earthiness from the nutmeg.

2 ounces mezcal

1 ounce pisco

½ ounce pineapple juice

¼ ounce agave syrup

Dash Liquid Smoke

Pinch ground nutmeg

Ice cubes

In a cocktail shaker, combine the mezcal, pisco, pineapple juice, syrup, Liquid Smoke and nutmeg. Shake with ice cubes, then strain into a coupe.

POUR ME ANOTHER

★ NOW TRY ★

Kicker Cocktail, 230

THIGRA

The rooftop bar at Hotel Casa Awolly in Mexico City is the sort of open-air affair where the city's sexiest seek to be seen. Luckily, the beauty at the bar is better than skin deep. Proof—their Thigra cocktail and its ability to blend the smokiness of mezcal with the earthy grassiness of matcha tea. I'm not a fan of green tea, so I was surprised I enjoyed this so much. The finished cocktail is tremendously refreshing. Their version uses lemon juice, but I found it overwhelmed the other flavors at home. Lime was far more friendly. The amount of matcha may not seem like much, but it's potent, so trust me on this one.

2½ ounces mezcal

½ ounce orange liqueur

¼ ounce agave syrup

¼ ounce lime juice

Generous pinch matcha tea

6 to 10 granules kosher salt

Ice, cubes and crushed

In a cocktail shaker, combine the mezcal, orange liqueur, syrup, lime juice, matcha and salt. Shake with ice cubes, then strain into a coupe filled halfway with crushed ice.

POUR ME ANOTHER

★ NOW TRY ★

Rum Old Fashioned, 229
Exposition Cocktail, 70
Vesper, 71
Fish House Punch, 216
Bull and Bear, 161
Oh, Henry! Cocktail, 162

MEXICAN VIEUX CARRÉ

The Vieux Carré is my daily drink, all strong and warm with hints of sweet and spicy. It's made with equal parts rye whiskey, cognac and sweet vermouth, plus a splash of Bénédictine and bitters. When I visited Limantour bar in Mexico City, I challenged mixologist Carlos Medina Piña to help me concoct a Mexican take on this New Orleans classic. His sub for the rye was brilliant—reposado tequila has similar rich, spicy notes. The cognac and sweet vermouth stayed the same. The Bénédictine would have, too, except the bar didn't have any. The solution? Just a spoonful of equally herbal-spicy Green Chartreuse. The result was simply amazing.

1 ounce reposado tequila

1 ounce cognac

1 ounce sweet vermouth

⅛ ounce (¾ teaspoon) Green Chartreuse

Dash Angostura bitters

Dash Peychaud's bitters

Ice cubes

In a stirring glass, combine the tequila, cognac, sweet vermouth, Green Chartreuse and both bitters. Stir with ice cubes, then strain into a coupe.

POUR ME ANOTHER
★ NOW TRY ★

Vieux Carré, 180
Vesper, 71
Oh, Henry Cocktail, 162
Dolce Vita, 133

LOADED PISTOL

This strong, herbal number—inspired by Erick Castro's original at Polite Provisions in San Diego—is a slow sipper. The mezcal is smoky, but takes on lovely herbal-sweet notes thanks to sweet vermouth and just a bit of Green Chartreuse. Grapefruit bitters add pleasantly hoppy notes and keep the cocktail from feeling too heavy.

2½ ounces mezcal

½ ounce sweet vermouth

¼ ounce Green Chartreuse

Dash grapefruit bitters

6 to 10 granules kosher salt

Ice cubes

In a stirring glass, combine the mezcal, sweet vermouth, Green Chartreuse, bitters and salt. Stir with ice cubes, then strain into a coupe.

POUR ME ANOTHER

★ NOW TRY ★

The Last Word, 72
Sazerac, 175
Well-Spoken Russian, 121
1920 Pick-Me-Up, 73
La Ultima Palabra, 256

CHARRO NEGRO

There is a whole family of cocktails that are little more than a liquor mixed with cola. The Rum and Coke. The Jack and Coke. Mexico's contribution? The Charro Negro, an icy blend of tequila and Coke, typically spiked with lemon or lime juice and often served on Día de los Muertos. The first time I tried it in Mexico City, I expected the worst. Except the sweetness of the cola offered a pleasant balance to the smoky tequila. I didn't care for any citrus; that just brought back bad memories of those strange Coca-Cola versions sporting lemon and lime. This generally is a tall pour—a bit of tequila and a whole lot of cola and ice in a highball. For my version, I dialed back the cola and added a splash of Ancho Reyes, a spicy Mexican liqueur made with ancho and poblano chilies.

2½ ounces blanco tequila

½ ounce Ancho Reyes

1 ounce cane sugar-sweetened Coca-Cola (usually sold in glass bottles—check the label)

Dash Angostura bitters

6 to 10 granules kosher salt

Ice cubes

In a stirring glass, combine the tequila, Ancho Reyes, cola, bitters and salt. Stir with ice cubes, then strain into a coupe.

POUR ME ANOTHER
★ NOW TRY ★

Cuba Libre, 218

LA ROSA

This is a much pared-down version of a cocktail I enjoyed at Chapulín, a Mexico City restaurant where chef Josefina López Méndez blends traditional recipes and ingredients with modern techniques. I loved her combination of smoky mezcal and vanilla-spiced Licor 43. To that, she added honey, citrus and jalapeño, but I found just a splash of orange liqueur and some orange bitters were plenty to balance things.

2½ ounces mezcal

¼ ounce Licor 43

¼ ounce orange liqueur

Dash orange bitters

6 to 10 granules kosher salt

Ice cubes

In a cocktail shaker, combine the mezcal, Licor 43, orange liqueur, orange bitters and salt. Shake with ice cubes, then strain into a coupe.

POUR ME ANOTHER
★ NOW TRY ★

Vieux Carré, 180

BUILDING THE BASIC BAR

The great thing about home mixology is that you don't need to spend a ton on gear in order to craft great cocktails. Here are the basics and how to use them:

2-OUNCE JIGGER

You will use a basic 2-ounce jigger every time you make a cocktail, whether shaken, stirred or simply sloshed. Skip bar-style jiggers, which resemble an hourglass. They are difficult to read and generally display fewer volume increments. Instead, opt for an inexpensive small liquid measuring cup, such as the OXO Mini Angled Measuring Cup, which offers volume measurements in ounces, tablespoons, and milliliters, and is easy to read and pour.

THE SHAKER

Opt for a large stainless-steel cobbler-style shaker with a volume of at least 2 cups/16 ounces, which can handle two or three cocktails. It has three parts: the cup, the top and the cap. The top has a strainer built in. Avoid Boston-style shakers (a large stainless-steel cup with a second, smaller cup that is inverted on top for shaking); they are tricky to hold and difficult to separate after shaking.

THE BASIC SHAKE

When shaking a cocktail, use about 1 cup ice cubes. Make sure the lid and cap are sealed. Hold it tight. Shake it for about 10 seconds for the proper chill and dilution.

THE DRY SHAKE

Working with hard-to-mix ingredients that need more than the standard shaking time? To avoid overly diluting the drink, do an initial shake—called a dry shake—of all ingredients without ice. Then add the ice and repeat for the usual time.

STIRRING GLASS

These wide, tall glasses make it easy to combine ingredients with ice and give them all a good spin. Most are sized to pair well with Hawthorne strainers (page 288). And they are tall enough to allow a vigorous stir without spilling. A 2-cup liquid measuring cup is a good alternative.

COCKTAIL SPOON

These long, thin spoons make it simple to stir cocktails in stirring glasses without splashing or plunging your fingers into the mix.

THE BASIC STIR

Depending on how long you mix it, a stirred cocktail generally is less diluted than a shaken cocktail. Aim for 8 to 10 seconds of stirring. If the drink needs to be strained (to remove the ice, herbs or other bits), do your stirring in a stirring glass. If no straining is needed—as in an Old Fashioned (page 131)—stir the ingredients directly in the serving glass. The biggest difference between stirring and shaking is that the latter dilutes and chills more, and often contributes tiny ice particles to the drink. These can be pleasant, but aren't always desired because they further dilute the drink as they melt.

THE STRAIN

Just as there are multiple ways to mix, there also are multiple ways to strain. Straining method is determined by mixing method and ingredients used.

THE BASIC

Most drinks need to be strained, if only to separate the liquid from the ice used during shaking; almost all drinks are served with fresh ice, not the ice used for shaking, which is broken up and will melt quickly, diluting your drink. If the only ingredients in the shaker are ice and liquid, use the built-in strainer that is part of cobbler-style shakers.

HAWTHORNE STRAINER

For stirred or shaken drinks with lots of fresh herbs or other large debris that might clog a cobbler's strainer, it's best to use a separate strainer. The easiest to use is the Hawthorne, which is a perforated metal disk with a wire spring around the edge to catch solids.

THE DOUBLE STRAIN

Drinks with a lot of pulp or seeds need to be double strained. A small conical or round mesh cocktail strainer is best, combined with either a cobbler- or Hawthorne-style strainer.

ALL ABOUT ICE

Ice cube size matters. A lot. Small cubes or crushed ice melts more quickly than large cubes, and for some cocktails that's fine. But in others that can mean overly diluted drinks.

LARGE CUBES For drinks you plan to sip slowly, use the largest possible ice cube. Silicone molds for making large cubes are widely available and inexpensive.

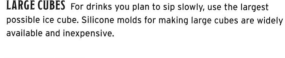

STANDARD CUBES Most of the recipes in this book assume you are using standard ice cubes. If so, two or three cubes per serving glass usually are plenty. Don't make the mistake of over-icing your drinks. Watery drinks taste as appealing as they sound.

CRUSHED ICE For crushed ice, a cloth Lewis bag and wooden mallet are great, but a heavy-duty plastic bag and rolling pin can bash ice pretty effectively, too.

MUDDLER

To get bold, intense flavor from many fruits, herbs and other tender ingredients, use a muddler (a long, thick wand with a blunt end) to lightly mash them in the shaker or stirring glass. Traditionally, muddlers are made from wood, but metal and plastic models can go in the dishwasher.

GLASSWARE

Sometimes glassware matters. Sometimes a drink simply needs the volume of a highball glass, or would look silly served in anything other than a rocks glass. So I usually suggest a style for each cocktail.

COCKTAIL GLASS

For when you're feeling fancy. Best for short pours.

COUPE

A squat cocktail glass. The go-to for many cocktails. The wide, shallow bowl allows you to fully experience the aromas of the cocktail.

HIGHBALL GLASS

Tall and thin. Also called a collins glass. Best for long pours with ice.

NICK AND NORA

Resembles a cross between a wine glass and a coupe. Best for short pours with no ice.

WINE GLASS

Not just for wine. Great for spritzers, and almost anything you'd serve in a highball glass. A stemless wine glass is a nice substitute for a rocks glass.

ROCKS GLASS

Short and thick. My glass of choice most of the time. Easy to hold and plenty of volume.

FURTHER DRINKING

My kitchen is home to an obsessive collection of cocktail books, including many mostly forgotten titles that date back a century or more. The internet is awash in affordable reprints of many of those and I highly recommend checking them out. In researching this humble volume, a particular pile of books new and old were invaluable. They include:

Bartenders' Manual by Harry Johnson, 1882

Cocktail Codex by Alex Day, Nick Fauchald and David Kaplan, 2018

Cocktails: How to Mix Them by Robert Vermeire, 1922

Death & Co: Modern Classic Cocktails by David Kaplan, Nick Fauchald and Alex Day, 2014

How to Mix Drinks by Jerry Thomas, 1862

Meehan's Bartender Manual by Jim Meehan, 2017

Modern American Drinks by George Kappeler, 1895

Mr. Boston Official Bartender's Guide edited by Anthony Giglio and Jim Meehan, 2009

Regarding Cocktails by Sasha Petraske, 2016

Rum: The Manual by Dave Broom, 2016

Schofield's Fine and Classic Cocktails by Joe and Daniel Schofield, 2019

Sip: 100 Gin Cocktails by Sipsmith, 2019

The Dead Rabbit Drinks Manual by Sean Muldoon and Jack McGarry, 2015

The Fine Art of Mixing Drinks by David A. Embury, 1948

The Flowing Bowl: When and What to Drink by William Schmidt, 1891

The Gentleman's Companion by Charles H. Baker Jr., 1939

The Ideal Bartender by Tom Bullock, 1917

The New Craft of the Cocktail by Dale DeGroff, 2020

The PDT Cocktail Book by Jim Meehan, 2011

The Savoy Cocktail Book by Harry Craddock, 1930

The World's Drinks and How to Mix Them by William Boothby, 1907

ACKNOWLEDGMENTS

Birthing a book begins as an intimate act, a ludicrous seed that takes lonely root in the nether regions of the writer's mind. As the seedling sprouts, the private notions and insecurities that eventually fill the page become increasingly public and shared. Suddenly, there it is for all to see and touch, and what once seemed so isolating becomes profoundly public. Along that journey, there are many who nudge and nurture. And to those, I am immensely grateful.

David Black and the entire troupe at the David Black Agency. You have a bad habit of not letting me finish one book before calling to demand the next. And for that, I am grateful.

Michael Szczerban and the team at Little, Brown. You saw promise in my insanity. Or maybe you just wanted a reliable source of fresh drinks to serve your wife. Either way, thank you.

Deborah Broide, public relations wizard and longtime friend. You worked nothing shy of magic and I can't thank you enough.

Lika Kvirikashvili, whose illustrations once again made my ideas come to life. Thank you for breathing such bold beauty into these recipes.

And Nicholas King, my husband and drinking partner. Thank you for always knowing the exact moment when a Vieux Carré is needed. Just in cases.

DRINKS INDEX

GENERAL INDEX

ABOUT THE AUTHOR

J. M. Hirsch is the James Beard Award–winning editorial director of Christopher Kimball's Milk Street. His previous books include *Shake, Strain, Done: Craft Cocktails at Home.*